MYTHS and TRUTHS
of the Cell Church

Key Principles that Make or Break Cell Ministry

JOEL COMISKEY, PH.D.

CCS Publishing
www.joelcomiskeygroup.com

Copyright © 2011 by Joel Comiskey

Published by CCS Publishing
23890 Brittlebush Circle
Moreno Valley, CA 92557 USA
1-888-344-CELL

All rights reserved. No part of this publication may be reproduced, stored in a retrieval system, or transmitted, in any form or by any means, electronic, mechanical, photocopying, recording, or otherwise, without the prior written permission of the publisher. Printed in the United States of America.

Cover design by Josh Talbot
Layout by Sarah Comiskey
Editing by Scott Boren

LCCN: 2011900362

ISBN: 978-0-9843110-7-1

All Scripture quotations, unless otherwise indicated, are from the Holy Bible, New International Version, Copyright ©1973, 1978, 1984 by International Bible Society. Used by permission.

CCS Publishing is the book-publishing division of Joel Comiskey Group, a resource and coaching ministry dedicated to equipping leaders for cell-based ministry.

Find us on the World Wide Web at **www.joelcomiskeygroup.com**

TABLE OF CONTENTS

Acknowledgements	9
Foreword	11
Introduction	15

Chapter 1: Vision Myths and Truths — 19
Myth: The Cell Church Strategy is a Mega-Church Strategy — 21
Truth: Few Cell Churches Reach Mega-Church Status — 22
Myth: The Cell Church Does Not Work — 24
Truth: Cell Church Brings Health, Life, and Growth — 25
Myth: Cell Church is a Fad — 26
Truth: The Cell Church Has Deep Roots — 26

Chapter 2: Model Myths and Truths — 29
Myth: Following a Particular Model Will Bring Success — 32
Truth: Apply Principles to Your Specific Situation — 33
Myth: The Number 12 Has Special Significance in the Organization of Groups — 35

Truth: The Principles of Evangelism and Discipleship Make Cell Ministry Work	35
Myth: Once You Have a Model, Stick by It	36
Truth: Innovate and Change the Model as the Spirit Leads	37
Myth: Cell Church Focuses Exclusively on the Cell and Celebration	38
Truth: The Cell Church Focuses on Key Systems that Produce Life in the Cell and Celebration	38
Myth: Change the Church by Criticizing It	40
Truth: Let People See It Worked Out	41

Chapter 3: Model Myths and Truths   43

Myth: Church Growth is the Driving Motivation for Becoming a Cell Church	46
Truth: Theology is the True Foundation upon Which to Build a Cell Church	48
Myth: If I Choose to Become a Cell Church, My Church Will Grow	52
Truth: Only Jesus Can Give True Organic Growth	52
Myth: If My Church Does Not Grow, I'm Not Successfull	54
Truth: Success Should be Measured by Faithful Effort, Rather than Results	54
Myth: The Cultural Context Should Dictate the Ministry Strategy	58
Truth: The Bible Critiques What Is Good and Bad in Each Culture	59

Chapter 4: Leadership Myths and Truths   63

Myth: Leading People into Cell Church Is Similar to Leading People into Other Church Programs	66
Truth: Leading a Cell Church Requires a Different Kind of Leadership	67
Myth: It's Okay to Simply Add Cell Ministry to What You Are Already Doing	69

Contents

Truth: A Pastor Needs to Make Cell Ministry the Central Priority 70
Myth: Lead Pastors Need to be Available to Everyone 71
Truth: Effective Cell Church Leaders Delegate 72
Myth: There Are Fewer Problems in the Cell Church than Traditional Ministry 73
Truth: Cell Church Ministry Reveals Problems Often Hidden under the Busyness of Traditional Ministry 74
Myth: All Pastors Must Lead Cell Groups 75
Truth: Not All Pastors Will Lead a Cell Group. Avoid Cell Church Legalism 76
Myth: If You Fail, Try Something Else 77
Truth: Failing Will Lead You to Discover What Works Best in Your Context 77

Chapter 5: Cell Focus Myths and Truths 81
Myth: The Cell Church Is All about the Cell 84
Truth: The Goal of the Cell Church Is to Make Disciples 84
Myth: View Everyone in the Church as a Leader 86
Truth: Everyone Should Be a Disciple-Maker 87

Chapter 6: Cell Group Myths and Truths 91
Myth: Cells Are an Extension of the Sunday Service 94
Truth: The Cell Is the Church 94
Myth: Cells Should Encompass All Small Groups 97
Truth: Start with a Quality Cell Definition 97
Myth: All Groups Must be Homogeneous 100
Truth: Allow Homogeneity to Naturally Develop as Cells Multiply 101
Myth: One Person Should Be the Designated Host 102
Truth: A Shared Hosting Arrangement Is Often the Best Option 103
Myth: Asking Everyone to Be in a Cell Stifles the Use of Spiritual Gifts 103
Truth: The Cell Group is the Best Place to Discover Spiritual Gifts 104

Chapter 7: Community Myths and Truths 107
Myth: Cells Are Only about Community 110
Truth: Cells Emphasize Community, Evangelism and
    Multiplication 110
Myth: The Cell Meeting Will Meet All the Needs 112
Truth: The Cell Meeting Is Only One Aspect of Community Life 112
Myth: The Cell Leader Should Develop All the Relationships
    in the Group 114
Truth: People within the Group Should Share the Relational Load 114

Chapter 8: Evangelism Myths and Truths 117
Myth: The Focus of the Cell is Entirely Evangelistic 120
Truth: Effective Cells Need a Strong Core of Believers 120
Myth: Evangelism in the Cell Church Is Only Relational 122
Truth: Don't Limit Yourself to One Evangelistic Method 123
Myth: A Cell Group Must Add a Certain Number of New
    Christians before It Can Multiply 125
Truth: Cell Members Should Evangelize but Avoid "Cell Rules" 126
Myth: If the Cell Emphasizes Evangelism and Multiplication,
    It Won't Grow in Community 127
Truth: Evangelism that Leads to Multiplication Enhances the
    Community in the Group 127
Myth: The Cell Leader Does the Evangelism 128
Truth: Each Member of the Cell Should be Involved in Outreach 129

Chapter 9: Multiplication Myths and Truths 131
Myth: All Cells Must Multiply within Six Months 134
Truth: Multiplication Rates Depend on Receptivity Levels 135
Myth: Shut Down a Cell Group That Has Not Multiplied
    within One Year 137
Truth: Keep Working with Cell Groups That Are Not Growing 138
Myth: A Cell Multiplies When It Reaches Fifteen People 139
Truth: Cells Multiply When a Disciple-Maker is Ready to Lead
    the New Group 139

Contents

Myth: When God Wants the Cell to Multiply It Will Do
    So Naturally   141
Truth: It's Best to Make Clear Plans for Multiplication   142
Myth: Multiplication Destroys the Relationships in the Group   143
Truth: Relationships Can Be Maintained after Multiplication   143

Chapter 10: Coaching Myths And Truths   145
Myth: Finding the Right Coaching Model Is the Key to Success   148
Truth: The Relationship between the Coach and the Coachee Is More
    Important Than the Structure   148
Myth: Coaches Only Listen and Ask Questions   149
Truth: The Coach Seeks to Equip the Group Leader with
    Whatever It Takes   150

Chapter 11: Transition Myths and Truths   153
Myth: Get Rid of the Programs Right Away   156
Truth: Wait until You Have Enough Cells to Cut Out Programs   156
Myth: Jump into Cell Church Immediately   157
Truth: It's Best to Have a Long Term Transition Plan   157
Myth: You Must Start the Transition with One Prototype   159
Truth: There are Various Ways to Transition   159

Chapter 12: Church Planting Myths and Truths   163
Myth: The Focus Should Be on the Success of a Singular Church   166
Truth: Planting New Smaller Cell Churches Is Desirable   167
Myth: The Church Starts When the Celebration Service Starts   169
Truth: The Church Starts When the First Cell Begins   169
Myth: Open the Celebration Service as Soon as Possible   172
Truth: Wait until There Are Enough People in Cells to Start
    Weekly Celebration Services   173
Myth: You Must Start a Weekly Celebration Service   174
Truth: Some Cell Churches Will Never Meet Weekly
    in Celebration   174
Run with Truth   175

Afterword	177
Appendix	181
Endnotes	185
Reources by Joel Comiskey	189
Index	197

ACKNOWLEDGMENTS

I'm the author of this book, but I've had plenty of help along the way. In the long process to make this book a reality, many hands and eyes have handled and contributed to the final work. Several people deserve special recognition.

Special thanks to Brian McLemore, World Bible Translation Center's (www.wbtc.org) Vice President of Translations, who once again critiqued my efforts, and the result is a better book.

Anne White offered her expert advice and thoroughly critiqued this manuscript, even editing the endnotes for mistakes and errors. Her insights were invaluable to the final draft of this book.

Bill Joukhadar made a special effort to look at this book and offer numerous suggestions and corrections. I treasure Bill's friendship and insight. His diligent effort made this book much cleaner and easier to read.

Rae Holt pointed out difficult phrases and especially encouraged me in the process. Patricia Barrett offered her wise counsel to the pages of this book.

My good friends and team members, Rob Campbell and Steve Cordle, both encouraged and challenged my writing. I really appreciated the time they took to look over this book.

Scott Boren, my chief editor, continues to do an incredible editing job. We've been together on twenty-one of my twenty-four books.

You'll notice that each chapter begins with specific insight from leading worldwide cell church thinkers. I'm so grateful that they took time from their busy schedules to make this book so much better.

Lastly, I want to thank my wonderful wife, Celyce, for being my best friend and providing the liberty and encouragement to write this book.

FOREWORD

Dr. Penrose St. Amant sat on the edge of his desk in 1957 to welcome the four of us who were entering the doctoral program in Church History he chaired at New Orleans Baptist Theological Seminary. Holding his arm out, he said, "Men, you have completed the training to pastor a church. Now you are entering a different Kingdom assignment: it is to view the *ecclesia* from an objective distance and speak prophetically into it. In order to do that, you must know the history of the church through the centuries. You then must fearlessly evaluate the contemporary church and call it to accountability for its activities. A false religious spirit breeds 'churchology.' Don't expect you will always be appreciated as you do this. Remember Martin Luther. He faced assassination when he challenged its corruption with his view of what it would take to reform the church."

Under St. Amant's mentoring, I began to inhale the life and spirit of Luther. I found he did not own his convictions: they owned him! The reformation of the church began when he discovered the just shall live by faith. Before the 95 Theses were nailed to the door of the Wittenburg church, Luther knelt and wept before the crucifix on the reredos, sobbing *"Mein Gott!*

Mein Gott! Fur Mich! Fur Mich! He had to change the life of the ecclesia to fit his new understanding of redemption.

Dr. Joel Comiskey is one of the men anointed by the Father to hold the cell church at arm's length, at an objective distance, to speak of the theology that breeds methodology. He has labored for many years in the trenches and has carefully written this book blasting the myths about the cell church. He has drawn from others who share the journey in each chapter to show the depth of what is truth among the myths.

Those of us who have held the traditional church at arm's length have grieved that we have robbed Christ of His true body. The modern cell church movement is founded on the conviction that we are "called out" to be inhabited by Christ, the Son. He will reveal His presence by manifesting His power working through us. We believe that the Holy Spirit has baptized us into "basic bodies" (cells) to expose small segments of society to His redemptive life. We believe that the primary instrument of evangelism is the simple observation by unbelievers of God working in us. We believe that we are all priests and connect God to man and man to God. We believe the five fold ministries described by Paul in Ephesians are the labor of mature believers who equip others for the work of their ministry.

This simply cannot happen in a church structure where people sit in rows to hear sermons and are not formed into basic Christian communities. The cell theology must become a replacement for the old wineskin, not a sewed-on patch.

I want to make one comment about the myths before you begin to read Joel's chapters. A "myth" is a polite word for "flat-out lie!" We are not playing ping-pong with church growth theories here; we are in warfare. Who is the enemy? He is called "the father of all lies, the Great Deceiver." Every myth is a satanic attempt to blind our eyes to truth. The refutations so effectively presented in this book is a call to commitment to the authentic church.

Thanks, Joel, for permitting the Lord to flow this book through your spirit and skills.

Ralph W. Neighbour

INTRODUCTION

I recently took my family on vacation in Yosemite and before leaving, I watched the PBS series on the U.S. National Parks. I learned that most of the Yosemite trails were created during the Great Depression when the national park service generated work for thousands of unemployed people. As we walked on cliff-hanging river trails and narrow mountain paths, I developed a new appreciation for the hard work of those early trail blazers who marked out the path for us.

The cell church also has its share of trail blazers. Moses followed Jethro's counsel and blazed a new trail of manageable groups of ten and supervisors of hundreds and thousands (Exodus 18). Jesus demonstrated the power of small group ministry by preparing his twelve in a cell and then sending them out to make new disciples (Matthew 28). The early Church laid down the pattern of celebration and cell by meeting in the temple and from house to house (Acts 2:42-46).

The church lost much of its vitality during the Constantinian era, but recaptured the biblical ideal through men like Philipp Spener, who prepared lessons from his Sunday sermon and distributed them to the weekly cell leaders. Spener was persecuted for changing the status quo of that time period.

Not long afterwards, Count von Zinzendorf, a disciple of Spener, took the small group concept further and instilled in his groups a missionary vision. These missional groups became known as the Moravian movement, the precursor of the modern missionary movement.

Perhaps more than anyone else, John Wesley pushed the cell movement forward by asking everyone to participate in a cell group as a prerequisite for membership. A person could not enter the celebration service without showing a ticket that he or she had participated in a small group during the week. Cell involvement, in other words, was the cornerstone of the Methodist movement.

David Cho is the modern day version of John Wesley in the promotion of life-giving cell groups. In 1966, Cho launched twenty home cell groups, led by women. From the twenty groups, the church grew to twenty-five thousand cells and two hundred fifty thousand people attending the mother church—easily the largest church in the history of Christianity.

Over the years, leaders have built upon the shoulders of these pioneers. Most of the modern day cell church movement is dynamic, positive, and applicable. As is true in most endeavors, errors and false assumptions also crop up to destroy an otherwise healthy movement.

I noticed that sometimes these false concepts caused the church to go astray completely. At other times, they led the pastor and church down a dead-end road of fruitless ministry. Often these errors or myths started with good intentions but grew into legalistic rules. Regardless of how the myths were generated, they had a chilling effect on the church's ministry. As a cell coach, I found myself spending more and more time trying to untangle the myths and half-truths and point the way to balanced, principled-oriented cell-church ministry.

I then began blogging on what I was seeing and eventually decided to teach the myths-truths in seminars around the world. Pastors and leaders responded with confirmation and appreciation, and I felt like I needed to take the next step and write them down into a book format, so more people could benefit.

My goal in this book is to help you avoid pitfalls and stay on the right path. I want to help you apply biblical, time-tested principles that will guide you into fruitful cell ministry. Whether you're starting out for the first time in cell ministry or a seasoned veteran, my desire is to give you the tools to help your ministry stay fresh and fruitful.

Each chapter begins with a unique twist. Around the world, there are great pastors and church leaders who have decades of wisdom in working with cell groups. They know the realities of these myths first hand, through the vice-grip of experience. I've asked some of these leaders to respond to a question about each topic in the form of an email, as if they are responding to a question from a pastor who wants to gather sage wisdom from a veteran. I am thankful for the time these leaders took to contribute to this book. I hope you enjoy their wise counsel.

One
VISION MYTHS AND TRUTHS

Dear Pastor Ben Wong,

As I survey the landscape of cell church leaders, few have the kind of experience that you offer. From the church in Hong Kong and the network of churches that you have helped foster, I'd like to know what you think about cell groups and church size. I know you work with all kinds of churches. Can you provide some insight into the goal of growing a large church?

Thank you for helping me out with this information.

Pastor John

Dear Pastor John,

There are a lot of huge cell churches in the world, and I have learned a lot from them over the years. However over 80% of all churches are under 100 members. Sadly, the focus is consistently placed on the biggest and most successful churches, and the smaller ones often feel like they are failures. Most of these pastors are very faithful people but find it hard to break the 100 barrier. Many of them are hurting because they feel that they have failed.

About fifteen years ago there was a lot of talk about group multiplication and how it would start off slowly and then gain exponential momentum. If you simply do the math you can see how this might work. Two groups become four. Four become eight. Eight, sixteen. Sixteen, thirty-two. Then 64. Then 128. I think you get the picture. The implication was that exponential growth was the expectation and that mega-size was the focus of the cell church.

Through the years, I think we have learned the fallacy of this approach. Years of experience have revealed that growth is not controlled by mathematical formulas. It's a lot messier than that. The fact is that some cells don't grow and multiply as you want. Some leaders get transferred to other parts of the world. Some get sick and can no longer serve.

But there are groups that grow and launch new ones. And this can lead to growth. But not all churches are going to grow large in size. In fact, the harvest is hindered when we assume that the big churches will have the primary kingdom impact upon a city. A network of smaller churches (under 150) could be the wise approach to take. So when a church grows from 70 to 160, the church could send out 25-50 people to start a new work.

Small churches matter. The fact is that research has shown it takes fewer people in a small church to lead someone to Christ than in a large church. So to assume the focus should be on growing big might just lead you down the wrong path. Instead think about the possibility of growing big by multiplying small.

I hope this helps,

Ben Wong, *founder of Shepherd Community Church and Cell Church Missions Network.*

Myth:

The Cell Church Strategy Is a Mega-Church Strategy

When I first started writing about cell churches, a steering committee directed me to study the largest worldwide cell churches because they were the most prominent. I was told that people would recognize them more readily and benefit more from my study.

I spent one to two weeks in each of these churches, which numbered into the hundreds of thousands of people and tens of thousands of groups. I conducted interviews, passed out a questionnaire, and tried to understand each particular model.

I then categorized the principles that each church had in common as well as what made them different.

I began to teach about the principles I saw in these large churches. However, in my teaching I gave the impression that the goal was to grow as large as these mega-cell churches. Several times during my early seminars people would challenge me about growing a large cell church. I would fumble a bit and respond that God wants church growth, and yes, he wills that our churches grow. I found it hard to mask my preference for large, growing cell churches. They had captured my attention, and it seemed like their example should stimulate other churches to expand their own vision.

I encountered one major obstacle, however. Practically all those in my seminars were from smaller churches. Many felt inadequate as I gave example after example of large cell churches. Whether I meant to or not, my underlying message was that growing large was a sure sign of success. Should growing into a large cell church be the goal?

Truth:

Few Cell Churches Reach Mega-Church Status

Most churches around the world have between fifty to one hundred people. According to the Hartford Study on North American churches, the average church in North America has seventy-five Sunday worshippers.[1] Even in Korea, the land admired for the world's largest churches, most churches are very small.

The fact is that the vast majority of pastors around the world are not called to manage a large celebration gathering. God has simply not gifted them to do so. Administrating such a large church involves managing details that most people are simply not equipped to handle.

My friend Ben Wong and I have often discussed the problem of smaller cell churches feeling inadequate when we have always emphasized the importance of mega-cell churches. Wong writes,

> Small churches comprise the great majority of churches in the world. Most pastors became pastors because they love God and desire to love his people. The reality is that in a small church, this can happen most effectively. In fact to become larger than 80 people, the pastor will need to become more administrative, and he may need a skill he does not have. Large churches need entrepreneurs, and very few pastors are like this.[2]

When we constantly promote large churches in our conferences, books, blogs, and articles, we give the impression that smaller churches are failures. They are not.

On one occasion I was asked to speak about cell church to key worldwide mission leaders of the Southern Baptist denomination at their headquarters in Virginia. They grilled me with questions about why the cell church movement focused on the few mega-cell churches, as if they were the norm. They desired a simpler, more reproducible strategy, one that didn't require large buildings, expensive lands, and large staffs. They were working in majority world countries and found that land was simply too expensive and money spent on buildings was counter-productive. They were looking for simple, reproducible strategies.

I agreed wholeheartedly with their assessment, also believing that the over-emphasis on mega-cell churches was ill-advised. I told them that ideally most cell churches would be small, simple, and reproducible. Some, I told them, however, would grow to a mammoth size, depending on the giftedness of the lead pastor and God's sovereign grace. I emphasized once again that such churches would not be plentiful, nor the norm; rather, smaller, more nimble churches should be the emphasis.

In my book, *Planting Churches That Reproduce: Starting a Network of Simple Churches*, I emphasize the need for smaller more reproducible cell churches that generate new church plants at a smaller size.

Smaller churches are here to stay. God has and will use them for His glory. Pastors who are planting cells, reaching the lost, making disciples, and planting new churches need to feel confident they are on the right track.

Myth:

The Cell Church Does Not Work

Many pastors see cell church as a strategy that might work in other cultures but not in their own. This is especially true in the western world. One church leader from North America wrote to me, "I was with a group of pastors the other day. One of the pastors, who is a church planter, said that cell ministry is not working in the American culture and its been generally set aside here in America. It works in other cultures, just not here." Many pastors echo the concern that cell church might work over there but not here. It's easy to look at the growing cell churches in other cultures and conclude that it won't work in my context.

Truth:

Cell Church Brings Health, Life, and Growth

Most pastors want more church growth than they are currently experiencing. Yet, in many places around the world there's a decline in spirituality and church growth in general. In the western world, this decline has been taking place slowly but surely for many years. David Olson's book, *The Crisis of the North American Church*, highlights the decline of church attendance in North America. Europe is even in a worse state. Ministry in the western world is hard.

The cell church strategy reminds church members that it's not enough to come to church on Sunday, hear a message, and then repeat the process the next week. Cell ministry helps members to live out the message during the week, be accountable to a smaller group of believers, and receive training to become a disciple-maker.

The good news is that cell churches have a better chance of surviving in resistant climates and actually growing more than non-cell churches. Natural Church Development did a worldwide study that used twenty million pieces of data to compare growth rates of cell churches with non-cell churches. The study found that cell churches grow 2.5 times faster than traditional churches and are healthier according to the eight NCD health factors.[3]

NCD applied the same data specifically to North America, and the results were the same. The study showed that cell churches overall scored significantly higher in all areas than non-cell churches. This study provides statistical evidence that cell churches—whether in North America, Europe, or Africa—grow both in quality and quantity.

This information gives hope to those who have doubted that the cell-church strategy could bring qualitative and quantitative growth to their churches. For those planting a church or whose congregation is in transition from a conventional church to a cell church, this study is a reminder that cell church ministry will actually provide a boost to celebration worship, church planting, and overall growth (see the appendix about this particular NCD study).

Myth:

Cell Church Is a Fad

Many look at cell church as a hot trend of the 1990s, but believe that there are now more cutting-edge strategies in the church. Some of the newer trends are multi-site ministry, seeker models, video venues, and so many more. Some think the cell church had its day but church life and ministry has largely passed it by; we should now focus on more promising developments.

Truth:

Cell Church Has Deep Roots

I was recently reading a book by Ron Trudinger called *Cells for Life: Home Groups, God's Strategy for Church Growth*. The author writes with penetrating clarity about the effectiveness of home cell groups and their power to transform lives and raise up new leaders. While reading the book, I had to keep on reminding myself that Trudinger is now in heaven, and he wrote the book in 1979!

There is nothing new under the sun. Home cell groups have been around for a long, long time. As I reflect on my own ministry, I'm keenly aware and appreciative of the pioneers who have gone before me.

Carl George's 1991 book, *Prepare Your Church for the Future*, revolutionized my own vision for cell groups and transformed my ministry. I stand on his shoulders. I'm also very grateful for Ralph Neighbour and Bill Beckham, two cell church pioneers, who have helped so many churches understand the values and principles behind cell ministry. Every time I read Neighbour's *Where Do We Go From Here?*, I receive new insight and grow in my appreciation for both the author and his in-depth cell church theology.

Going back even further, we see David Cho, the founder of the modern day cell church movement. I have never fully recovered from reading Cho's *Successful Home Cell Groups* back in 1984. It lit a passion inside me for the possibilities of home group ministry. But Cho didn't start the cell church movement. He stands on the shoulders of John Wesley and the Methodist movement, who were helped by the Moravians, who in turn were heavily influenced by the Pietists. And all of them stand on the New Testament's emphasis of house to house ministry and celebration worship (Acts 2:42-46).

The modern day cell church movement is not new. It's actually quite ancient. I'm grateful for the pioneer work of Ron Trudinger and others.

While we in the present day cell church movement ask God for future insight and direction, we are very grateful that cell church is not a fad. Cell church is here to stay.

Two
MODEL MYTHS AND TRUTHS

Dear Pastor Mario Vega,

I am not new to pastoral leadership, but I am relatively new to the world of the cell church. I have read about your cell ministry at Elim and am amazed by how God uses your church. I have a few questions about how to find the right cell church model. Do you have any counsel?

Thank you for your time,

Pastor Cliff

Pastor Cliff,

Cell ministry is exciting, and your search for input is admirable. Too many just jump in without asking hard questions. Here's my perspective:

Don't do cell groups solely because of numerical growth. While other pastors strive to copy successful models from other churches, you must not lose sight of the fact that the key to cell success is not following a model but following values and principles.

When talking about values, I'm referring to biblical truths. For example, in the Bible, we find teachings on the priesthood of all believers, love for one another, and all the one-another commands (e.g., edify one another, pray for one another, exhort one another, confess sins to one another, and so on).

And then there are those principles that have been learned through the experience of putting cell ministry into practice. I'm referring not only to the modern day cell church movement (some fifty years of experience) but also to the Anabaptist churches, the Puritans, the Moravians and Wesley's church. All did cell groups differently, but they shared common values and principles.

The models emerge from the application of the values and principles to a particular church context. Models respond to the cultural contexts, and therefore, are children of times and circumstances. What was valid at one time will not necessarily have significance in another time and place.

It can be useful to study cell models to obtain ideas and insights, but there will always be certain elements that will not apply in your culture and context. Because of that, you must be very creative and develop your own model. Models are not transferable, but the values and principles are indeed valid in every place and time. The values hold true because they are taken from the Bible. Principles can also be applied because they have been identified in many places and at different time periods. The models, however, respond to a specific place and time.

Once you develop your own model, you must keep perfecting it because it will surely need improvement. As you continue working on it, you will be able to make the adjustments you consider necessary. All cell models are adjusting and permanently updating themselves. I would be careful, however, about major adjustments. In other words, do not change from one model to another one. If you do, you are no longer focusing on the values and principles but on the model itself. It is also a sure way to discourage the church because the members will be confused and will become turned off to the cell vision.

What is the fundamental purpose of cell work? It is to return to live out the values and the principles of the New Testament Church. Assimilate the values and principles. Meditate on them, live them, adjust your mentality to them, and then, God will give you your own model in his time. The secret to successful cell work is that there is no secret; success comes when we live the values of the New Testament church.

Many Blessings,

Pastor Mario Vega,
pastor of Elim Church, El Salvador and Elim International.

Myth:

Following a Particular Model Will Bring Success

I consulted a church who followed the Groups of Twelve model, developed in Bogota, Colombia. I discovered that before jumping into the G12 camp, they were following Cho's model, and before that they copied the Saddleback model. Now waving the G12 flag, they were trying very hard to copy the model exactly.

They even took trips to the International Charismatic Mission in Colombia and made similar pilgrimages to other famous G12 churches. They wanted to catch the anointing of these churches, so they could experience similar growth. In spite of their high expectations, their church did not grow.

As I talked to this pastoral team, it became clear they were neglecting basic cell fundamentals in the hope that the model would automatically produce growth. I noticed little flexibility and an unhealthy focus on outward structure that didn't suit their culture, denomination, and background.

These pastors are not alone. Many pastors covertly or overtly believe that finding the right model will unlock their success. They might have heard the pastor of a growing cell church say something like, "All you have to do is follow what I'm doing and your church will grow." You are then instructed to come back multiple times to learn the correct procedures. But is choosing and following a model the best way to proceed?

Truth:

Apply Principles to Your Specific Situation

Many pastors just don't understand that principles—not models—produce fruitfulness. The growing cell churches are innovative and break the molds. David Cho, for example, became convinced of the cell model on his death bed. He realized that Jethro's advice to Moses in Exodus 18 applied to his own situation. He then read about the house churches in the book of Acts, and God gave him the vision to start home groups. He had to innovate and tweak his structure as he went forward because he was pioneering new ground. He followed the Spirit of God based on what he saw in scripture.

The Elim Church did something similar. They became excited about cell ministry after visiting Cho's church in Korea, but they realized that they had to adapt to the Salvadorean culture. Cho's exact model didn't work for them. They decided that each cell needed a weekly planning meeting to prepare for the cell group. This weekly planning meeting met in addition to the weekly cell meeting and all cell members were encouraged to attend. This was one of the keys that unlocked cell fruitfulness in their own culture.

Principles take precedence over models. Principles allow for flexibility and apply to a wide range of situations. Models are culturally bound.

Models are inflexible and often require an exact set of circumstances to make them work. Principles apply to any denomination, culture, or situation.

In my study of cell churches around the world, I discovered several common patterns or principles:

1. Dependence on Jesus Christ through prayer.
2. Senior pastor and leadership team giving strong, visionary leadership to the cell ministry.
3. Cell ministry promoted as the backbone of the church.
4. Clear definition of a cell group (weekly, outside the church building, evangelistic, pastoral care/discipleship, clear goal of multiplication).

The above four are the most important, but I noticed other common principles in these growing cell churches:

- The passion behind cell ministry is reaching a lost world for Jesus Christ.
- Reproduction (multiplication) is a major goal of each cell group.
- Cell and celebration attendance expected of everyone.
- Required cell leadership training for all potential cell group leaders.
- Cell leadership developed from within the church itself, at all levels.
- A supervisory, coaching care structure for each level of leadership.
- Follow-up system of visitors and new converts administered through cell groups.
- Cell lessons based on pastor's teaching to promote continuity between cell and celebration (although flexibility might be given to meet the needs of specific homogeneous groups).

The principle approach allows for plenty of adaptation and innovation. In fact, I admire pastors who have adjusted their cell ministry to better fit their own context.

Rather than being the slave of someone else's model, pastors should follow principles and become a fresh, vibrant example in their own context.

Myth:

The Number 12 Has Special Significance in the Organization of Groups

The International Charismatic Mission in Bogota, Columbia exploded with growth in the 1990s and became a worldwide sensation. I wrote about their church in my book, *Groups of Twelve: A New Way to Mobilize Leaders and Multiply Groups in Your Church*. I later had to pull back my support for this church because of their fixation on the number twelve and their exclusivity in promoting their own model. Was ICM's model based on the number twelve the secret to their success?

Truth:

The Principles of Evangelism and Discipleship Make Cell Ministry Work

The International Charismatic Mission became effective by following certain principles rather than a particular number. One principle they perfected was seeing every person in the church as a potential leader—not only those with the gift of evangelism or the gift of leadership.

Since ICM saw the potential of cell leadership in every member, the logical step was to train each person to participate in cell ministry. Much of their training involved breaking bondages and liberating people from sins that held them back.

ICM also saw every leader as a potential supervisor and asked each parent cell leader to supervise the cells they birthed. Because supervisors were not appointed in the G12 model, each individual leader had more motivation to multiply cell groups.

Sadly, ICM fell into the trap of asking everyone to follow their entire model, rather than principles that could be adapted and adjusted according to context. They began to promote their entire model as being the only anointed one. They asked churches to adopt their model rather than adapting principles. My advice is to adapt G12 principles rather than to adopt the G12 model.

Myth:

Once You Have a Model, Stick by It

When a church follows cell church principles over time, it might become an example for others to follow. Other pastors might visit, ask questions, and even participate in the church's network. Once a church has arrived at this point, is it best to stick with the exact strategy that has produced that growth?

Truth:

Innovate and Change the Model as the Spirit Leads

A church never arrives at perfection. There is always room for improvement. The moment, in fact, that a church thinks it has arrived, it probably has already begun its downward spiral.

John P. Kotter, a business professor at Harvard University, wrote a book called *A Sense of Urgency*, in which he says:

> Complacency is much more common than we might think and very often invisible to the people involved. Success easily produces complacency. It does not even have to be recent success. An organization's many years of prosperity could have ended a decade ago, and yet the complacency created by that prosperity can live on, often because the people involved don't see it.[4]

One of Kotter's main points is that complacency that comes from success is the enemy of progress. Of course, Kotter is writing to businesses, but churches fall into the same trap.

Churches often lose the urgent dependency on Jesus Christ when things are going well. They become content with their models, buildings, and other outward signs of success. They forget the sense of urgency that brought their fruitfulness.

When a church arrives at what it considers to be the optimal point of growth and fruitfulness, the temptation is to stay there, rather than pressing on to new heights and gaining new territory. I was in one cell church whose leaders didn't want to write down their structure because they were changing and adapting continually. "We are following the Spirit of God and changing daily according to God's plan," the youth pastor said to me. I realized that the secret to their success was depending on Jesus.

One of the secrets of Elim's continual fruitfulness over time is their practice of precise statistical accountability. They don't hide anything. Each week, Elim knows exactly what's happening in the cell system, and they are able to make rapid changes when weaknesses are spotted.[5]

Those churches who continue to bear fruit over a long period of time depend on God, point people to reproducible principles, and make mid-course corrections.

Myth:

Cell Church Focuses Exclusively on the Cell and Celebration

Many have likened the cell church to a two-winged bird. Just as a bird needs two wings to fly, cell churches thrive on both cell and celebration. Cells meet together during the week, but then those cells come together to celebrate on Sunday.

Two-winged comparisons are made so frequently that many people don't realize that cell churches need additional supporting structures to function effectively. What are those additional systems?

Truth:

The Cell Church Focuses on Key Systems that Produce Life in the Cell and Celebration

Besides cell and celebration, other systems make cell church work. The two main ones are training and coaching.

Training

Cell churches have a step-by-step process to take a person from conversion to spiritual maturity. The training track is intimately linked with cell ministry and furthers the process of cell multiplication.

Synonyms for the word "track" include path, route, channel, and road. An equipping or training track takes the new believer from point A to point B. The training is specific, and the end result produces disciples who make other disciples through new cell groups.

Cell church training tracks feature clarity and "doability." They have a definite beginning and ending and a new person entering the church can readily understand what it takes to go from A to B.

Coaching

One of the key differences between groups that start and fizzle and those that make it over the long haul can be summed up in one word: coaching.

Even the best of the best need a coach. Michael Jordan needed a coach. Jordan's coaches spotted the opposing team's strategy, defended Jordan against over-zealous referees or players, and knew what drills and skills Jordan needed to improve. A coach sees the big picture and can help the player reach his or her full potential.

Most churches can successfully start groups—even hundreds of them. People will even readily offer their homes—for a few weeks.

To make it over time, however, the small-group leaders must have a high-quality support system, much like the supply line that channels food and other materials to battle-weary soldiers.

The cell-driven strategy succeeds or fails on the quality of the coaching given to the cell leaders.

Myth:

Change the Church by Criticizing It

Jesus saved me at seventeen, and when I was nineteen I joined a miracle ministry called Shekinah Fellowship. Brant Baker was the leader of Shekinah, and the ministry prospered for a number of years. As the months went by, however, I noticed that Brant Baker's message was increasingly negative against the church. I constantly heard, "The church is dead and God's miraculous power through Shekinah is the answer." Soon after this wave of negativity, Shekinah lost its way and folded.

Years later, I noticed another popular ministry making negative remarks about the church of Jesus Christ. Once again, I heard the repeated message that the church had failed, and now this new ministry was raised up to revive Christ's ailing church. Like Shekinah, this ministry grew rapidly and then declined when the founder died.

Some in the cell movement excel in putting down others, while exalting the cell structure as the new wineskin. They construct a "us-them" mentality. Everyone else is doing ministry wrongly and the only group doing it right is the cell church. Many, in fact, embrace the cell church because they are disillusioned with the conventional church. Yet can negativity sustain the cell church movement?

Truth:

Let People See It Worked Out

Churches and ministries lay a very weak foundation with a negative message. Granted, scripture critiques our lives and ministry and never sugar coats the truth. Yet, once the theological foundations for cell ministry are laid, people need a positive message of how to implement that biblical message in their own culture and context.

I've spent a lot of time doing cell church ministry in Brazil and have heard testimony after testimony of churches who have applied cell principles and seen wonderful fruit. Their fruit encouraged other Brazilian pastors to press on. Testimonies like this do wonderful things. They give others a window into something real, something that's been worked out in the hard knocks of life.

Just do it. Let people see the results in action. I personally believe that cell church ministry is the best strategy out there. Yet, I realize that it's not the only strategy, and that God is using various ministries to bless his body and grow his church. God has supernaturally placed me in his body to encourage and fine-tune cell church ministry.

All those living under the Lordship of Jesus and committed to his inerrant word are part of his organic church. Leaders in Christ's church need to be very careful about badgering and bad-mouthing Christ's blessed body.

Three

CHURCH GROWTH MYTHS AND TRUTHS

Dear Bill Beckham,

I want to thank you for your books. Your way of thinking challenges us to think deeply about how we do church. Yet, I still have questions about church growth. Are cells the best way to grow the church? It seems like some people make church growth the focus of the cell church? Do you have any insight?

Thanks for your time,

Pastor Hector

Pastor Hector,

Yes you are correct. A lot of the focus of small group and cell church literature is about how to grow your church. They focus on huge mega-churches, as if that should be the goal of every church. I don't have a problem with growth. We need churches to grow, but the focus is not on growing huge mammoth church organizations, buildings, and budgets. That won't work for most churches. We need to develop a different approach for growth that takes our focus off size. For instance, instead of building huge cell churches that depend upon traditional large group worship services, we should consider other alternatives that facilitate a different kind of growth, but remove the focus from how many gathered at the same building. Let me offer such an alternative.

The current public worship and teaching model may work for some larger existing churches, but it presents problems for church planting and the expansion of existing small churches. A new large group model should be low maintenance, inexpensive (escapes the building problem), flexible, and transferable, while allowing for high growth.

Jesus modeled a large group alternative in Luke 10 when he trained the seventy. Instead of a large group gathering focused on public worship and teaching, he opted for a tactical equipping model. With this large group he did the following things. He:

- *set the rules for their engagement,*
- *deployed them,*
- *debriefed them,*
- *interpreted their experience.*

Traditional models focus resources (time, treasure, energy) on worship and teaching programs that require expensive buildings, a large work force and produce consumer Christians. The Luke 10 large group training model focuses resources on equipping, mentoring, conversational learning, prayer, and debriefing.

Jesus' Luke 10 large group model can be configured along with small groups and a public large group to fit the stage of development of a church plant or existing small church.

Stage 1: Small groups, plus a periodic Luke 10 large group for training, sending and forming.

Stage 2: Small groups, plus a regular Luke 10 large group for training, sending and forming.

Stage 3: Small groups, a regular Luke 10 large group plus a periodic public large group.

Stage 4: Small groups, a regular Luke 10 large group and a regular public large group.

If we want to see growth, we must not make attendance growth the focus. We must move away from making the head count at a public large group worship service the main thing. Equipping people for ministry will lead to true growth as we refuse to tie up our best leaders in doing lots of stuff to run high-maintenance worship events. Invest your time in exploring other alternatives and finding ways to invest in your people, so that they can minister.

Bill Beckham,
Author of numerous books, including <u>The Second Reformation.</u>

Myth:

Growth Is the Driving Motivation for Becoming a Cell Church

In the early years of my cell church research, I became enamored with the cell church concept because of its potential for church growth. I noticed that the largest churches in the world were cell churches, and I visited many of them to discover patterns and principles. The rapid growth of these cell churches and my own church growth philosophy were like a match to gasoline. Church growth ignited my soul with a deep passion for cell ministry.

As a missionary in Ecuador, I formed part of the pastoral team in one of the key mission churches, and my new role became the director of small groups. Eventually we began to implement cell ministry and saw the church explode. The mother church planted a daughter church, and I participated on the church planting team. We saw the same incredible growth in the new church.

Around that time, I criticized certain leaders in the cell church world for focusing too much on values and theology. I thought they were slowing down the cell church process by emphasizing biblical foundations more than church growth. My mission was to place cell church squarely within the church growth camp.

At that time, I prided myself in pragmatism. I had studied the largest cell churches in the world and could now tell everyone how to quickly grow a cell church.

However, I was faced with one huge problem. I realized that certain countries could count on church growth because the Spirit of God was already moving. Cell church ministry enhanced and fed the flames of the growth already happening. The growth, in other words, was coming from the Spirit of God, rather than from the cell church strategy.

For example, I was in Bogota, Colombia, in 1997 with Ralph Neighbour. We were there to check out a large cell church, which was breaking church growth records. While I was impressed with their growth, I also realized that many other non-cell churches were also growing rapidly. A particular pastor from England noticed the same thing. He was visiting Colombia at the same time and happened to visit a nearby non-cell church that was exploding with growth. He testified to us about the amazing growth in Colombia in general.

I discovered the same truth while in Ecuador. Our cell church exploded, but many other non-cell churches were also growing rapidly.

In 1999 while living in Ecuador, I conducted a five-week seminar in five different U.S. cities. Different cell churches hosted each seminar, and I was dumbfounded by the lack of growth in these churches. I was accustomed to the rapid growth taking place throughout Latin America, so I thought these North America cell church pastors were doing something wrong.

During my five-city tour, I showed the attendees photo after photo of growing cell churches, hoping I would stir them to greater vision. Rather, they gave me a "deer in the headlights" gaze. They just didn't know what to do with these worldwide church growth claims. It just wasn't happening here in North America.

In 2001 I came back to North America to coach cell church pastors and plant a church. People were not as receptive and were busy with work, material things, and life in general. Most were not eager to join a cell group, get involved in the training track, or volunteer for cell leadership. I discovered rather quickly that I could "grow a church" much faster by asking for less commitment.

The more I travel on my cell church journey, the more I see that the cell church strategy doesn't produce rapid growth. God reserves growth for himself. He wants to receive the glory for all church growth. By his grace, he doesn't allow man to glory in himself. God wants to get all the glory.

Then why should a pastor be enticed to implement the cell church strategy?

Truth:

Theology Is the True Foundation upon Which to Build a Cell Church

Ralph Neighbour repeatedly says, "Theology must breed methodology." This phrase was one of Neighbour's central themes in his 1990 book, *Where Do We Go from Here?*. As I write in 2011, twenty-one years after Neighbour wrote this book, I've arrived at the same conclusion. The good news is that the cell church strategy is rooted in a strong biblical theology.

Biblical truth is the only firm foundation for anything we do. Without biblical truth, we don't have a firm under-pinning upon which we can hang our ministry and philosophy. We can plow through most anything when we know that God is stirring us to behave biblically.

Cell church is not the latest, greatest church growth strategy. If it were, it would simply be a passing fad until the next hotter, more relevant strategy comes along. In many places around the world (like the West) cell church transforms the church through a purification process. Church growth is slow but cell church helps Christ's church go deeper.

What are some of the key biblical truths that cell church brings out?

Making Disciples

Christ's last command to his disciples was to make disciples of all nations. I believe the essence of cell ministry is making disciples who make disciples. Cells are leader breeders and the best place to prepare disciple-makers. Multiplication is at the heart of cell ministry because new cells provide the environment for making new disciples. The goal of the cell church is to raise up an army of leaders to continue the work of Christ's church.

Evangelism

God took the form of a human being, so he could reveal his love and character. Jesus said that he had come to seek and save the lost. His ministry on earth was to heal the broken hearted and to set the captives free. Following Christ's example, cell evangelism is primarily relational. Cells penetrate society, bring good news of the gospel to the hurting and needy, and continue the process through multiplication.

Priesthood of all Believers

Some churches grow large through filling pews. Yet, scripture teaches that all believers are priests. Cells value the participation of every believer.

Part of the priesthood of all believers is the use of spiritual gifts. I've written various books on this topic and believe that cells provide the best atmosphere for spiritual gift use.[6] In fact, all of the New Testament gift passages were written to house churches.

Community

Our God is a social God. He's in constant unity with the other members of the Trinity: Father, Son, and Holy Spirit. He is not an individualist. Jesus demonstrated that unity while on earth, never doing anything that wasn't perfectly pleasing to the Father and Spirit (John 5:19-30). He then told his disciples to walk in that same unity. He said the best witness to an unbelieving world was the love and unity that existed among the disciples (John 17:6-26).

He wants us to be involved in community, which flows from his very nature. Cell ministry promotes the wealth of one-another ministry found throughout the Bible. Through cell church ministry, the Triune God is challenging an individualistic mindset and asking his church to die to self and practice the one-anothers of scripture.

As I've ministered in North America for the last ten years, my thinking has radically shifted from the question, "How can cell church work in North America?" to "How can we obey scripture that tells us to live in community and do life together?" There's a huge difference between the two convictions. One is based on pragmatism, the other on scripture.

Theological Operating System

Some of you reading this book might remember the old Windows DOS operating system back in 1991. Microsoft started off with DOS, a code-based operating system, and then tried to marry it with Windows, an image-based system. For a short while, a user had to buy a version of Windows that ran on top of the DOS system.

My marriage of cell church with church growth was like placing Windows over DOS. I simply placed cell church on top of church growth.

DOS was my church growth paradigm, the code of my old thinking. When I discovered cell church, I placed cell church thinking on top of my church growth paradigm. Cell church was like Windows 3.1, Microsoft's first attempt at the windows operating system.

I discovered, however, that church growth theory was sadly lacking. It was a great operating system in countries that were receptive and focused on growth. It was sadly lacking in non-receptive cultures that needed revival.

Theology is the best operating system for all of life, including cell church ministry. Trying to place cell church over another strategy, like church growth, is clumsy and simply doesn't work well. I have now changed my cell church paradigm structure. I'm no longer placing it over my church growth philosophy, like Windows over DOS. I now believe and teach that biblical theology provides the best framework and motivation for doing cell ministry. I now realize that growth or lack of growth is not the reason to do cell church. Biblical truth is the only firm reason to run with the cell church philosophy.

The Cell church challenges assumptions about the church. It stirs believers to think more deeply about the Christian life. Is Christianity simply an event to attend? Or is it a lifestyle to live? In many hardened soils around the world, the cell church is a challenge to truly live out the claims of Christianity. It challenges time commitments and what is really important in life.

The only reason why someone in a materialistic culture would make a commitment to attend a cell, enter the equipping track, and even become a multiplication leader or coach (all volunteer ministry) is because Jesus Christ has touched his or her life.

The cell church, therefore, in many countries around the world, is a counter-cultural challenge to become the people of God and the Church of Jesus Christ.

Myth:

If I Choose to Become a Cell Church, My Church Will Grow

Many people join the cell church movement because they've heard about Yoido Full Gospel church, the Elim church, or one of the other growing cell churches around the world.

They jump into the cell church strategy due to a promise—stated or unstated—of church growth. The underlying assumption is that if I become a cell church, my church will grow.

I confess that I gave this impression in my early days of cell ministry. If a pastor or church did cell church correctly, their church would grow. I've since become acutely aware of how easy it is to fall into this technique-driven methodology.

Truth:

Only Jesus Can Give True Organic Growth

I'll never forget walking at Myrtle Beach, South Carolina in February 2008. As I walked on the sand, I reflected on my experience of cell church growth in Ecuador and North America.

I had come to realize that the structure called cell church didn't have power in itself to grow a church. At that moment while walking on the sand, I envisioned the cell church as a giant kite. The kite just sat there on the sand, and it couldn't move without the wind picking it up. People could walk by and admire the kite, but it couldn't fly into the air without the power of wind.

I realized that many cell churches are like that beautiful kite. They are well polished and beautifully constructed. The system is carefully laid out. Yet, the church won't soar by itself. It will just sit there. A pastor can't force the kite to take off. Unless the wind of the Spirit breathes into the structure and causes it to fly, nothing is going to happen. Apart from the Holy Spirit, church growth won't happen. In fact, it should not happen. The only growth glorifying to God is the type that he initiates.

Jesus said, ". . . on this rock I will build my church, and the gates of Hades will not overcome it." Jesus Christ is the head of the church. All authority has been given to him (Matthew 28:18). He will build his church, and he is the only one who can sustain that growth.

The senior pastor cannot grow the church. Cells cannot grow the church. Programs cannot grow the church. Because it is Christ's church, he must grow it. The only type of growth worthy of Christ's church is the supernatural, God-inspired growth.

We can plant and we can water, but ultimately God must give the increase (1 Corinthians 3:6-9). We should not want to be part of a church that grew because of the senior pastor's skill or personality. Can you imagine the pressure on such a pastor to keep the church growing? (Many of the major pastoral scandals were caused by this human pressure to perform.) As soon as church growth becomes a man-made "I did it" strategy, we should flee.

Some pastors are so desperate for growth, it seems like they'll do anything to make it happen. I heard about a church in Texas who gave away fifteen brand new cars during the Easter service. Attendance was at an all-time high that day! I suppose the attendance increase that day could be called church growth, but it's probably best to take the word "church" out of the equation. Call it a raffle, an event, or a car drawing. Simply gathering people into a group or crowd is something other than the New Testament church. Even Jesus while on earth attracted multitudes to his miracles, but then he asked them to count the cost and most faded away.

The bottom line is that Jesus won't be manipulated to give growth to a church, no matter how desperate. The good news is that Jesus is in charge of the church, and he wants us to come to the point of looking to him for growth, so that we can point to the miracle of his growth rather than a slick set of programs that were implemented to make it humanly happen.

Myth:

If My Church Does Not Grow, I'm Not Successful

A dreadful disease has permeated cell church ministry. It's called "Yonggi Cho envy" or "big church envy." Cho is just the personification of what I'm referring to because his church is so large. Pastors and churches experience a lot of jockeying to have a larger church than the next guy. The result of this attitude is that many pastors feel like failures when their churches don't grow.

Truth:

Success Should be Measured by Faithful Effort, Rather than Results

Church growth generally teaches that God rewards workers who reap, rather than those who faithfully sow the seed. This is called "harvest theology." Again, it downplays the Christian teaching that God rewards faithfulness and uplifts those pastors and churches who are experiencing growth. Because I was committed to this church growth thinking, I found myself pressured and pressuring others to produce.

After one year of planting the church in California, I hired an associate pastor from South Africa who was a precious brother and thoroughly committed to cell ministry. At that time, I was traveling around the world and expected this pastor to make things happen and grow the church. I was following the church growth teaching that places the responsibility on the pastor to grow the church. My thinking was that if the church grew, it was because of the effectiveness of the pastor. It if didn't, the pastor had problems.

The associate pastor from South Africa eventually left, and this time we hired a senior pastor to replace me. I found myself doubting the new pastor when the church didn't grow as expected. I wondered if this new pastor was the right guy.

Finally, a board member confronted me saying, "Joel, what are you doing? You're never satisfied. I'm not ready to go through another change because I believe our new pastor is God's man for this church."

God spoke to me. I realized that my pressure was human driven. About that time I read the book *Evaluating the Church Growth Movement, 5 Views*. One view was the traditional church growth view. The other three views were modified understandings of the traditional church growth view, set forth originally by Donald McGavran. The fifth view, promoted by Gailyn Van Rheenan, critiqued church growth on the basis of theology. I found myself agreeing wholeheartedly with Dr. Van Rheenan. God spoke to me that I needed to judge church growth based on what the Bible says and not the other way around.

About that same time period, I realized that if I was doing everything possible to reach out and minister, I was successful in the process of doing this.

Yes, we have to plant; we have to water; we have to do our part. Yet, ultimately, God must give the increase. When he does give the increase, we can rejoice in his supernatural blessing and goodness. If he doesn't give the increase, we continue to be faithful, knowing that God honors our diligent effort and service.

We are successful in the process of being faithful. God asks us to make the very best effort possible under his guidance. As we are led by him, we are successful in the process of planting, discipling, and watering. We look to him for the increase, but we are successful whether we see the fruit or not.

I ministered in a cell church in the Midwest. The church was a model of cell church growth for a number of years, but then it stagnated. The founding pastor felt like he should be seeing growth each year and began to feel like a failure when the growth stopped. I was very impressed with the life and excitement in the church, but the pastor was discouraged. "I'm fed up," he told me. "I've just lost interest. Maybe I should be doing something else."

I preached in his church on Sunday and was encouraged by God's work in the church. But once again the pastor began to condemn himself because the church wasn't growing each year. He told me that he felt like a failure and that perhaps he should simply leave the church. I listened intently, but eventually I found myself saying, "Who brings the growth? You do many things well, but you have a problem in trusting God to bring growth in your church. You need to hang in there until it happens." His wife, knowing I hit a raw nerve, encouraged him to listen closely.

Many pastors don't hang in the saddle long enough. They don't trust God's sovereign hand to bring the growth and give the eventual victories. They leave too early.

Is there a time when God calls pastors and leaders to move on? Yes. However, moving on when feeling like a failure is not the best time to move. My counsel is to hang in there. God wants to reach lost souls and make disciples more than we do. Yet, leading a church is often more about what God wants to do in the life of the pastor. When the pastor has matured, the growth appears. Our job is to plant, water, and put in the best effort possible.

I spoke at a seminar with Mario Vega in Guatemala a few years ago. Mario is the lead pastor of the Elim Church in El Salvador, one of the largest cell churches in the world (over one hundred thousand people in cells). Three church planters came up to me after the seminar to ask whether they were on the right track because their church was struggling and not seeing the incredible fruit that Elim was experiencing. These pastors were faithfully laboring and sowing precious seed, but they had become discouraged by their lack of results.

I took these three church planters aside and strongly encouraged them. I told them that they were doing an amazing work and that God would give the growth in his timing. I reminded them of Galatians 6:9, "Let us not become weary in doing good, for at the proper time we will reap a harvest if we do not give up."

I prayed over them for God's anointing and when I looked up, I noticed several of them crying. They just needed to hear that they were on the right track.

If you are faithfully doing what God has called you to do, you are also on the right track. Hang in there. God will grow his church in his timing.

Myth:

The Cultural Context Should Dictate the Ministry Strategy

The theory of church growth promotes that pastors and leaders must first understand the culture and then create strategies that will help the church grow in that particular culture. According to this view, understanding culture and then creating strategies based on that culture, is the key to church growth.

Cultural sensitivity, of course, is good and right. Paul also promoted cultural relevance when he said,

> Though I am free and belong to no man, I make myself a slave to everyone, to win as many as possible. To the Jews I became like a Jew, to win the Jews. To those under the law I became like one under the law (though I myself am not under the law), so as to win those under the law. To those not having the law I became like one not having the law (though I am not free from God's law but am under Christ's law), so as to win those not having the law. To the weak I became weak, to win the weak. I have become all things to all men so that by all possible means I might save

some. I do all this for the sake of the gospel, that I may share in its blessings (1 Corinthians 9:20-23).

Is it possible to take cultural relevance too far? Should methods that work to grow the church become the determining factor about what church strategy a pastor or church should adopt? Because it works, people assume that it much be blessed of God. This is not always the case.

Truth:

The Bible Critiques What is Good and Bad in Each Culture

Being accountable to other believers, living out the Christian life, and then inviting non-Christians to join is simply biblical. When we win people to Jesus, we must win them into the biblical, one-another lifestyle. It's not a question of whether this ministry "works" in a western context. Rather, the question should be, "Is it right?"

Cell church cuts across the grain of individualism. It challenges the church to live a New Testament lifestyle of community. It shouts loudly that Sunday attendance is only half of the equation. Lifestyle change takes place in an accountability structure where people are growing in relationship with one another.

Writing the book, *Relational Disciple*, was very hard for me. I was biased against what I considered an over-emphasis on community in the small group movement in the western church in general and in North America more specifically. I had dedicated much of my earlier writing to cell evangelism and multiplication and became convinced that the "community emphasis" of many small group ministries was an excuse not to reach out.

Yet, as I struggled through the writing of that book, I realized that I didn't have the option of accepting or rejecting community. Scripture simply didn't give me that option. The Bible, in other words, is chalked full of references to community. Jesus repeatedly told his disciples to love one another and that the unbelieving world would come to faith in him through their unity (John 13).

The one-anothers are woven throughout scripture and there are more than fifty Bible references that teach believers to serve, wait, care, give, and in general, practice community. I had to submit to the Bible's clear teaching, even if it went against my pre-conceived notions.

God showed me that all cultures have good and bad points. Some cultural traits are in accordance with scripture, while other aspects need to be corrected by scripture.

For example, in some cultures, bribery is common. Some might say, "To make it in our culture, we have to bribe." One pastor in Russia told me that police set up check points and will take away your license unless you produce a bribe. I felt sorry for this pastor and have no idea how awful it would be to live in a culture like this.

Regardless of the cultural norms, however, scripture teaches that bribery is wrong.[7] Many verses speak against it. Thus, we can say confidently that this aspect of culture needs to change to conform to scripture and not the other way around. It doesn't matter if everyone is doing it. It's simply wrong.

I consider myself part of the North American culture, even though some people consider Californians as part of a different planet. Some traits of North American culture, such as diligence and adherence to the rule of the law are clearly scriptural and backed by many verses in the Bible. Other North American traits, such as individualism, need to be critiqued by the clear teaching of scripture.

Most in North America don't give their individualist tendencies a second thought. But are they scriptural? Scripture is clear when it talks about community, the one-anothers of scripture, walking in unity, hospitality, and many other New Testament norms. Joseph H. Hellerman, professor at Talbot Seminary, wrote a book called *When the Church Was a Family*. His conclusion is that the New Testament culture was group oriented and that God instructs us to live like a family.

The biblical norm is not individualism but mutual ministry and a group oriented lifestyle. Becoming relationally oriented is painful to individualists. We want to do our own thing. Yet, scripture, not culture, must determine who we are and what we do.

Four
LEADERSHIP MYTHS AND TRUTHS

Dear Dr. Les Brickman,

I have been following your ministry for a few years now. I see how God is using the church in third world countries, and I'm thankful for you and your wife, Twila, who are dedicated to serving those churches. I've also noticed that you have done a lot of work to understand how leadership development works in a cell church. Do you have some insight in this matter that you could share?

Thank you,

Pastor Jeff

Dear Pastor Jeff,

When I work with pastors, I often hear them say something like this: "I really am committed to cells. I believe they are biblical. They are the heartbeat of our church. However, you need to understand, I am not very relational. Certainly you cannot expect me to change who I am, or how I live my life and lead the church. I have put so much time and effort into growing the Sunday service, and it is hard to focus my energies now on cell ministry. I am a visionary, but not a very detailed person. That is why I have left the details of implementation to others. Besides, you must agree that I have to balance my oversight of our cells with all our other current programs."

Cell church leadership understands that transformation happens experientially. Consider the cost of leading a cell church. Not what it will cost your leaders, but what it will cost you! Me? Yes, you! Cutting edge you say? Ready to follow the vision you say? Sadly, you can possess great vision and lead a regular church without a radical change in your underlying values and lifestyle. Leading a cell church demands the transformation of values and the alteration of lifestyles. Relationship becomes a core value, as do authenticity and accountability. Individual activities can no longer be nicely slotted into convenient time slots in your Google calendar. Time demands are too great and slots are too few. The challenge becomes learning how to integrate all the time demands of a new cell lifestyle, while maintaining balance. If, as cell leadership, we cannot model a new transformational lifestyle, we can forget leading a cell church where we say, "Follow me as I follow Christ."

Cell church leadership understands we learn from life's experiences as we pause and reflect back over both our "successes" and "failures." Leaders in conventional churches are expected not to "fail." That is, after all, why they are leaders. Success is trumpeted; failure forgotten. As cell church leaders, failure in the kingdom becomes redefined as we learn from our experiences, make necessary changes, and move forward. We are not leaders because we make fewer mistakes, but because we learn and grow from those we make. This understanding permeates even the cells, so they become safe environments in which we may stumble and learn how to walk in the Spirit's gifts.

Cell church leadership is not about giving everyone the answers, but believing in your people to the point that you draw out from them what God has placed within, empowering them to fulfill their destiny and place in the body.

Experiential transformation. Learning from life. Believing in your people. Three marks that set apart cell church leadership. I hope this helps you on your journey.

Les Brickman,
D.Min., author of various cell church books. He is currently a missionary in Kenya.

Myth:

Leading People into Cell Church Is Similar to Leading People into Other Church Programs

Most pastors have experience in starting new programs such as AWANA, Evangelism Explosion, Vacation Bible School, or a new program from their denomination.

Programs normally have a built-in life-cycle which can be discontinued after a semester, one year, or when the church decides to change programs. Many pastors approach starting cell church ministry in a programmatic way. They want to take it out of the box, set it up, and then delegate others to make it work.

They view the cell church strategy as a technique or program that can be used for a time and then discontinued.

Truth:

Leading a Cell Church Requires a Different Kind of Leadership

Cell church is not another program. Rather, it focuses on people. Pastors need to consider the new challenges this strategy will have on how they lead the church before they begin the journey into cell life.

Steep Learning Curve

Most pastors have been trained in seminaries that taught the traditional model of the paid pastor who does the work of the ministry. It's not easy for pastors and congregations to prepare lay people to do the work of the ministry and then to coach them to make sure they fulfill their pastoral ministry.

Extra Work Required to Train and Coach Leaders

The cell church asks potential leaders to go through a specified training. In fact, all members are encouraged to take the training. Those who become cell leaders (or part of the leadership team) need on-going coaching. Pastors need to realize this and count the cost to make sure training and coaching takes place.

Misunderstanding from People with Other Agendas

When a church moves forward with a vision, there will always be people who attack it. Whenever a leader goes in a particular direction and asks people to follow, some will resist, preferring another direction or keeping things just as they are.

Finding Leaders Who Will Be on the Same Page

It's one thing for the senior leader to be on board, but it's also critical that every member of the leadership team also supports the vision. When this happens, a team can go forward together. The cell church is really all about leadership development and the leadership team is the steering wheel of the cell church. If the leadership team is united and guiding the cell church vision, there's a good chance the rest of the church will follow.

Losing People

Richard Houle caught the vision to transition his conventional French-speaking Baptist church in Granby, Quebec to the cell church vision. He believed in the theology behind the cell strategy and realized that the new direction required commitment and change. In the process, sixty people left the church. Houle continued to press on out of obedience to God's calling.

As the years passed, the church reached new people and began to produce fruit. Eventually, they became a cell church planting movement with four daughter churches connected to the mother church. When I visited them in 2009, I was thrilled to see Richard Houle's apostolic role over the four daughter churches and especially how Houle's example had positively impacted his entire Baptist denomination. A large number of denominational leaders came to my cell seminar because of their relationship with Richard Houle and his French-speaking congregation.

Ramon Justamente is a southern Baptist pastor in Florida. He counted the cost to become a cell church by studying the literature and visiting various cell churches (he and his wife even visited our cell church in Quito, Ecuador in 1999). He was totally convinced he should transition his church.

I don't think Ramon was ready for what happened next: four hundred people left the church. Yet, Ramon believed God had called him to cell church ministry, and he wasn't going to back down.

When I held a seminar in his church ten years after the transition, I saw a vibrant cell church. God has not only won back far more than four hundred who had left, but the people were excited, motivated, and serving Jesus with zeal and passion. I spoke on how to transition a church, and Ramon gave his testimony.

If Ramon was just "testing the waters" he would have only lasted a few months. His commitment to the vision and values of cell church ministry helped him to "weather" the violent storms and stay afloat when things got rough. Ramon's church is now a great model for those doing cell ministry in Florida.

Both Houle and Justamente could not foresee all obstacles, but they were convinced of the Biblical foundation of cell ministry. They never viewed cell ministry as a technique that could be discarded if it didn't work. Rather they viewed it as a biblical way of life.

In *The Challenge of the Cell Church*, Phil Potter details his own journey of transitioning a traditional Anglican church in England to the cell church model. Potter guided his congregation to grasp the cost involved before jumping into cell ministry. They spent months planning and preparing for the transition. Because he faithfully counted the cost, Potter was able to start cells that continued to grow and multiply.

Phil Potter exemplifies the need for careful planning and counting the cost before plunging into cell ministry. Jesus encouraged similar planning when he challenged people to count the cost to follow him. He warned the crowd of the danger of starting and failing to finish (Luke 14).

Cell church is not a program. Pastors who have successfully planted or transitioned to the cell church model have done their homework and are ready to stick with it for the long haul.

Myth:

It's Okay to Simply Add Cell Ministry to What You Are Already Doing

Most churches have a lot of things going on. Over time, the church has developed a myriad of programs and ministries.

Suddenly the pastor hears about cell church, gets excited about it, and adds it on as another one of many programs.

Or perhaps the church is doing well, but the pastor has heard of the amazing growth of cell churches around the world and wants to see if cell church strategy will help his church grow even more. So the church includes the cell church agenda on top of what the church is already doing.

When the cell church strategy fails to produce the desired growth, the pastor deletes it from the schedule as he would any other program that didn't seem to work.

The pastor might even become a critic of the cell model, saying it doesn't work or it's not right for their particular church culture. Yet upon further analysis, the normal reason for abandoning cell church ministry is a faulty understanding of what it takes to make cell ministry work.

Truth:

A Pastor Needs to Make Cell Ministry the Central Priority

We can't emphasize everything equally. Some pastors try so hard to help everyone that they wind up helping no one. The phrase "concentrated focus" is critical to make cell ministry work.

People will only do a few things well. If the pastor wants them to be involved in cell ministry, he can't also expect the people to be involved in many other church activities.

Are programs bad? No. It's simply a matter of choosing the focus. We all know how cluttered and busy our lives are. If the pastor expects his people to choose cell ministry, this means they will need time to visit neighbors, attend a cell group, prepare the cell lesson, go to the coaching meeting, and other related activities.

The word *no* is a blessed word in the cell church. Only the lead pastor can stand up and say *no* to all the well-intentioned programs that arrive at the church door.

In December 2010, I held a seminar in Pastor Samuel Mejia's church in Santa Ana, California. The church has one hundred forty cell leaders and planted five churches. Pastor Samuel realized he had to focus on cell ministry and make it his priority.

Most of the churches in Samuel's denomination are program driven. Samuel stands out from the crowd because of his "concentrated focus" on cell ministry. Because pastor Samuel has persisted for twenty-five years, many churches in his denomination are now following his example. Why? Because they've seen it worked out in his church. Pastor Samuel is a great example of concentrated focus.

Myth:

Lead Pastors Need to be Available to Everyone

When I took a course on pastoral theology in Bible school, my professor taught us the conventional model of church ministry. The called, paid pastor was supposed to do the work of the ministry. He was available for everyone and everything.

Some pastors fit right into this model. They entered the pastorate to preach, marry, bury, counsel, and to be available to those with needs. They love to teach large groups of people—

anyone who is willing to come, sit, and listen. These pastors live for the celebration service. They feel worthwhile when preaching to a group of people.

When someone walks into the church for counseling, they are ready to receive him or her, even when others are available to counsel the person.

Some pastors simply don't have the vision to delegate and mentor other leaders to do the work of the ministry. Rather, they prefer to do it all themselves.

Truth:

Effective Cell Church Leaders Delegate

Jethro's advice to Moses was to choose leaders to care for groups of tens, fifties, and hundreds, so that he would not have to carry the load by himself. Jethro summed up the problem succinctly, "You are wearying yourself and also those who hear you" (Exodus 18:18). Moses tried to be a responsible leader, but it was too much for him to do alone.

Cell church ministry requires delegation. Cell church pastors who make it over the long haul empower the members to do the work of the ministry. They pastor the flock through others. Ephesians 4:11-12 says, "It was he who gave some to be apostles, some to be prophets, some to be evangelists, and some to be pastors and teachers, to prepare God's people for works of service, so that the body of Christ may be built up."

Except for visionary leadership, effective cell pastors delegate almost everything else to others. Not all pastors are able to do this. Perhaps they don't know how. Or maybe they don't want to. After all, there's a certain power in being the "go to" person. I personally know some pastors who like to take every counseling appointment that comes through the church. Members expect the pastor to do all the work of the ministry.

The goal of the pastor whose church is based on cells is to equip the members to carry on the work of the church. When the sheep have a problem, effective cell pastors ask if they have first talked with their cell leader. They refuse to pass over the cell leaders in the process of caring for the sheep.

I've done numerous seminars with Mario Vega, the senior pastor of Elim San Salvador, one of the largest churches in the world. Pastor Vega has learned to stay focused. He concentrates on caring for the top level cell pastors who care for others. He participates by directing the top leadership to make cells work every day.

Effective cell church pastors make sure the vision is fulfilled through delegating the work to others. Moses didn't have to do everything, but he did need to make sure things were accomplished. He did need to oversee the ultimate delegation of responsibility. Jethro's advice to Moses freed Moses up from having to stand and listen to the entire nation all day and night. It also helped the people under his care to go away satisfied.

Myth:

There Are Fewer Problems in the Cell Church than Traditional Ministry

Throughout this book I've extolled the virtues of cell church ministry, while not trying to hide its problems. A lot of pastors gravitate to cell church ministry because of those positive points. Yet, there's a danger in giving the impression that cell church ministry will wipe away all the church's problems.

Truth:

Cell Church Ministry Reveals Problems Often Hidden under the Busyness of Traditional Ministry

I spoke in a church in Puerto Rico. One wise elder said to me that before cell ministry, problems were always below the surface, but the since they began to emphasize cell groups, those problems came to the light. People were free to share about them. Suddenly, there were far more problems. "The good news," he told me, "is that we are now dealing with those issues."

When a pastor focuses on cell ministry, people have the opportunity to share what's going on in their lives. Demonic strongholds and psychological problems will often surface. Those problems were always there, but no one noticed them. They were below the surface. While the people sat in the pews, everything seemed great. When the people have the freedom and opportunity to share what's happening in their lives, it seems like the church is full of problems.

One person who attended my cell was living with another woman. He attended the large celebration service of two churches but no one knew about his personal life. When he joined my group, it became apparent that he was not married. He had a desire to follow God and realized he needed to change. Over time, he repented, got involved in the equipping track, and made steps to change his situation. He stopped living with this woman, entered pre-marital counseling, and eventually married her. They later opened a cell group.

In his book, *The Apostolic Cell Church*, Lawrence Khong writes,

For years I successfully pastored a traditional Baptist church. It was relatively easy to organize the church around worship services, Sunday school classes and various fellowships for various age groups. Most of the activity centered on teaching within a classroom. The biggest challenge most of the time was to make a good presentation, be it a sermon or a class lesson. The situation is far more demanding for a cell church.[8]

When Khong says "far more demanding," he's referring to getting to the root of people's problems and helping them change. The good news is that the lead pastor doesn't have to solve all church problems. His main role is to equip leaders to pastor the church and help others become like Christ.

Myth:

All Pastors Must Lead Cell Groups

When a pastor is leading a cell group or part of a cell leadership team, he has additional authority with his congregation. The pastor is able to connect the message on Sunday with the needs of the person in the congregation.

God first showed me this truth while in Ecuador. I had just returned to Ecuador after researching growing cell churches around the world. I discovered one glaring weakness: all the supervisory roles in the cell church world were removed from cell life. A fruitful leader left the cell battle to supervise those on the front lines.

At the Republic Church in Quito, Ecuador, we decided to change this. We asked all members to lead a cell (or co-lead) while coaching a network of cell groups. We had far more authority, and the respect of the other cell church members because we stayed on the front lines. And because it worked so well, I encouraged pastors to lead cell groups in all my writings and seminars. Yet must all pastors lead cell groups?

Truth:

Not All Pastors Will Lead a Cell Group. Avoid Cell Church Legalism

Some pastors do not lead cell groups and still are great visionary leaders.

The Bible is silent on the subject about whether a pastor must lead a cell group. Where the Bible is silent, we also must be silent. As mentioned earlier, I used to push this concept very hard but have since backed off. While I still feel it's a great idea, sometimes it's best for a lead pastor to lead a cell group for a time and then spend a season in coaching the cell leaders or in a larger church, the coaches of leaders.

At other times, the lead pastor might decide it's best to simply attend a cell group or form part of a cell leadership team.

Jamey Miller, who started his church plant by leading a cell, took a break from cell leadership. But then he decided to jump back into cell leadership to stay in touch with people in his neighborhood.

While I encourage pastors to lead a cell group, there are other alternatives to stay in the battle.

Myth:

If You Fail, Try Something Else

I know pastors who tried cell church ministry, failed at it, and then became cell church critics. They say, "Oh yes, I tried cell church, and it didn't work." Or they might say, "Cell church works great in Latin America but not here in my city." But often these pastors didn't keep trying. They were not willing to make mid-course corrections, such as seek out a coach, visit another cell church, or read relevant cell church literature.

Truth:

Failing Will Lead You to Discover What Works Best in Your Context

Whether making mistakes or total failure, pastors who make it in cell ministry keep pressing on and don't give up. They practice the title of John Maxwell's book, *Failing Forward*. Making mistakes is part of life. We rarely get things right the first time. Often we don't do them right the third and fourth time either. In fact, we grow and mature through the trials and errors we make. Failure is the back door to success and God will bless our efforts.

Henry Cloud and John Townsend wrote an excellent book called *Boundaries*. They say,

> He [God] wants us to be assertive and active, seeking and knocking on the door of life. God's grace covers failure,

but it cannot make up for passivity. We have to do our part. The sin God rebukes is not trying and failing, but failing to try. Trying, failing, and trying again is called learning. Failing to try will have no good result.[9]

You have to fail more than once before you get things right. Proverbs 24:16 says, "For though a righteous man falls seven times, he rises again, but the wicked are brought down by calamity."

The cell church equipping track, for example, is rarely perfected the first time. A pastor and leadership team has to make numerous auto-corrections to perfect the equipping track. The same is true for any part of cell ministry such as coaching, vision casting, keeping statistics, setting goals, evangelizing, and disciple-making.

Whenever I think of giving up, I'm encouraged by those who overcame failure through persistence:

- When Thomas Edison invented the light bulb, he tried over two thousand experiments before he got it to work. A young reporter asked him how it felt to fail so many times. He said, "I never failed once. I invented the light bulb. It just happened to be a two thousand-step process."
- Winston Churchill failed sixth grade. He did not become prime minister of England until he was sixty-two and then only after a lifetime of defeats and setbacks. His greatest contributions came when he was a "senior citizen."
- Albert Einstein did not speak until he was four years old and didn't read until he was seven. His teacher described him as "mentally slow, unsociable, and adrift forever in his foolish dreams." He was expelled and refused admittance to the Zurich Polytechnic School.

- After years of progressive hearing loss, by age forty-six German composer Ludwig van Beethoven had become completely deaf. Nevertheless, he wrote his greatest music—including five symphonies during his later years.
- Rafer Johnson, the decathlon champion, was born with a club foot.
- Babe Ruth struck out one thousand three hundred thirty times, but he also hit seven hundred fourteen home runs.[10]

Don't worry about failed outcomes. Worry about the chances you miss when you don't even try. Most good things come through testing and making mid-course corrections. If you wait to try until everything is perfect, you most likely will never get there. "But wait a minute," you might say. "I want everything to be perfect before I try." Sorry it doesn't work that way. We learn from our mistakes.

Five

CELL FOCUS MYTHS AND TRUTHS

Dear Pastor Abe Huber,

It seems that your church has really learned how to make cell groups work. I've read a ton on the subject and gathered lots of opinions, but I'd like to hear your perspective from the point of view of an experienced pastor. I want to shepherd my people better and lead them into cell groups, but I don't want to force them into a structure against their will. Do you have any counsel?

Many Blessings,

Pastor Marcus

Dear Pastor Marcus,

I sense you have a pastor's heart, and that you really want to care for your people. At the same time I am sure that you would like to reach more people for Jesus. Well I have good news for you. If you truly disciple the people God has given you, they will naturally attract new people to the flock. Healthy sheep naturally give birth to baby lambs!!

From my experience, the key to great cells is great discipleship.

The big question is: "How can we guarantee that all will be cared for and truly discipled?" To begin a process of discipleship in your church, you have to take the lead and be an example. First of all, you as the pastor need to have a mentor/discipler with whom you are accountable for your spiritual life. I'm referring to someone who will pray with you and give you counsel. This person should be someone who you look up to, who is also respected by your congregation, and who gives you spiritual covering.

Once you have a discipler, it is always a lot easier to encourage the whole church to want to be discipled. You should then start discipling some of your key men, one-on-one. Spend quality time with them, helping them with their relationship with the Lord, and in their relationship with their family.

As this discipleship continues, you will be able to truly mentor these men (one-on-one, and in a group setting). In your discipleship times, you will be asking a lot of questions about their disciples, and you will help them bring spiritual health to their disciples.

It is also very important that your key disciples become leaders and supervisors of your cells. Your discipleship time with them will include mentoring them on how to effectively lead, multiply, and supervise their cells.

Supervisors disciple cell leaders, and cell leaders disciple apprentices. Apprentices will disciple cell members, and cell members will disciple other members.

You and your disciples have to remember this: Our priority is not to multiply the cells. Rather, cell multiplication is the natural outgrowth of effective disciple-making. Our priority is to make "disciple-making disciples." As leaders we should be reproducing new leaders. If your disciples are cell leaders, and if they are being effective in their discipleship, they will definitely be reproducing new cell leaders!

Lovingly, I have to remind you, however, that you can only reproduce in others what has first been produced in you. You can only give birth to new leaders, if you humbly permit someone to speak into your life and allow the "birth pangs" of Christ to be formed in you. You will only be a good discipler, if you first become a good disciple. That is why it is so crucial that you model discipleship. Your key leaders and members of the church will also want to be discipled and mentored as they see how much you value your discipler and receive from him.

I believe that this is just the beginning of a discipleship revolution that will transform you and your ministries!

I pray God's blessings on you,

Pastor Abe Huber, Senior Pastor of Igreja de Paz, a cell church of fifty thousand with an additional five hundred churches in the network.

Myth:

The Cell Church Is ALL about the Cell

Most people would never accuse the cell church of not focusing on the cell. After all, those within the cell movement agree that the cell is its crown jewel. All other cell systems spring from the cell, and it deserves a central role. But is it possible to become too enamored by and focused on the cell? Are there other more important priorities?

Truth:

The Goal of the Cell Church Is to Make Disciples

Scripture is clear in Matthew 28:18-20 that the church is called to make disciples. Jesus never told the church to go and start cells. Rather, he told them to make disciples in all nations.

Some people think I'm too fanatical about cells. I surprise them when I tell them I'm not passionate about cells in and of themselves. Rather, my focus is on making disciples. God's purpose is to make disciples who make other disciples.

So what does this have to do with the cell? I believe the cell is the best vehicle to make disciples who make other disciples (multiplication).

Jesus himself modeled this truth to the world when he chose twelve men and then lived in a small community with them for three years. He discipled his twelve in an environment where he could give plenty of practical instructions and interact with them. Much of Christ's teaching was show and tell, and as the disciples matured, they were able to lead the church.

The disciples continued to make other disciples in that same environment. When the Spirit of God descended on the day of Pentecost, the disciples were in the upper room of a house in Jerusalem. The Spirit came down in a powerful way, and the disciples of Jesus began to meet from house to house. Believers met in houses where they could love one another, practice hospitality and continue the work of Jesus. Although their time with the Master influenced them to meet from house to house, it was also part of their Jewish heritage from the time of Jethro's counsel to Moses to break up into groups of ten.

The same disciples who were nourished in house-to-house ministry spread the gospel by planting house churches and connecting them to celebration gatherings when possible (Acts 2:42-46).

The cell has all the elements necessary to raise up ministers. Cells are mini-churches. Effective cell leaders pastor, evangelize, train, counsel, encourage, listen, and challenge Christ followers. Those who lead cells do what pastors do.

Jesus came not to be served but to serve and give his life as a ransom for many (Mark 10:45). Leading a cell is all about giving, even when people don't give back. It's about exercising *agape* love without expecting anything in return.

I don't know of a better environment to make a disciple who makes other disciples than cell ministry. The context of the cell is a far more effective way to train future disciples than the large celebration atmosphere. Speaking, singing, or giving an announcement before a large crowd can be a frightening experience. It's not a place to experiment and make mistakes.

Programs and ministries in the church do not train disciples effectively. They don't emphasize life-transformation and value change, like the relational, give-and-take environment of a small group. In the cell, everyone can minister and in fact, is a minster. John said in Revelation 1:5-6, "To him who loves us and has freed us from our sins by his blood, and has made us to be a kingdom and priests to serve his God and Father—to him be glory and power for ever and ever! Amen."

In the cell group, members learn how to reach out to non-believers, counsel an erring member, listen to the needs of others, or visit someone who hasn't attended recently. The cell environment allows a person to minister to others and in the process grow personally.

Myth:

View Everyone in the Church as a Leader

Many of the growing cell churches ask each person to enter the training track to eventually become a leader. I immediately saw this as a positive development over the goal of attendance and promoted it in my first book *Home Cell Group Explosion* and then later in *Leadership Explosion*. After all, Jesus said in Matthew 9 that the harvest is plentiful but the laborers are few. Raising up new cell groups is a great way to raise up new leaders. But should everyone become a leader?

Truth:

Everyone Should Be a Disciple-Maker

In 2001 I started coaching pastors in cell-based ministry. One particular pastor was a gifted teacher. He was very analytical and wrestled with the word *leader*. He didn't accept pat answers from me but wanted to make sure that cell ministry was biblical and that the terms also came from the Bible. We as a coaching group wrestled for hours about the word *leader*.

Dave felt that the word **disciple** squared with scripture far better than *leader*. I had been using the word *leader* for so long and even entitled one book, *Leadership Explosion*. Yet, I had also been growing disillusioned with the word because so many misinterpret the leadership role as the person who controls and dominates.

Jesus transformed this notion by telling his disciples that the greatest would be one who served the most (Luke 22:26). He took off his garment and washed the feet of his disciples to model servanthood. But many people forget this and think of leadership in terms of power and authority. Many then shy away from a "leadership role" because they feel inadequate.

I've come to the conclusion that rather than trying to reinterpret the word leader continually, it's best to use a more biblical term, like *disciple* or *harvest worker* to describe leadership in cell ministry.

I was confronted with this issue when coaching Jim Corley, a pastor in Tucson, Arizona. The mission statement of CrossPoint Community Church (CCC) was to prepare disciples who make disciples, although they didn't really have a way to define what a disciple looked like.

Pastor Jim Corley and I both agreed that a disciple is a follower of Christ, but we needed to know how that would look practically in the cell church paradigm. Corley and his key leaders were uncomfortable with the idea that a disciple was only a cell leader, and I understood their discomfort.

God gave us wisdom to break down how a disciple could be defined in the cell church paradigm. I recommended that the church define a disciple in the following way:

- D-1 disciple (member of a cell and the equipping track). The first step is for a person to be in a cell and participate in the training track. In this process, the person is baptized and taught to obey all the things that Christ has commanded (Matt. 28:18-20). Key steps in the training process include doctrinal teaching, holiness, baptism, evangelism, and preparation to minister to others.
- D-2 disciple (active participation in the cell group) The next step is for the disciple to practice what he or she is learning. The term D-2 disciple defines a person who is in a cell, taking the next step in the training track, and actually helping in the cell group. Such a person is playing a significant role in the cell group.
- D-3 disciple (cell leader or part of a cell leadership team). The next step is for the disciple to gather people together and lead a cell group either individually or as part of a team. The disciple has gathered friends and family and is facilitating the cell group or is one of the leaders on a cell planting team. He or she has graduated from the training track.
- D-4 disciple (multiplication leader). This is when the cell leader has developed another disciple who is leading his or her own cell group or part of a cell leadership team (has gone through the D-1 to D-3 process). I would call a multiplication leader a D-4 disciple.

Of course the D numbering doesn't have to stop with a D-4 disciple. In fact, Jim Corley added the role of church planter and pastor. The main purpose for D1-4 is to more specifically define what a disciple might look like in the cell church.

Take my own men's cell group. Matt came into the cell as a D-1 disciple. He accepted Jesus as a child but only recently rededicated himself to Jesus. Matt became a D-2 disciple as he went through the training track and actively participated in the cell, including leading the cell on multiple occasions. When Matt completed the training, I turned the group over to him, and he became a D-3 disciple. At that point, I became Matt's coach. We would love for Matt to continue the process and eventually multiply another disciple to facilitate a new cell group, thus becoming a D-4 disciple.

In 1 John 2:12-14, John talks about the progression from faith as little children to a mature father's faith. Discipleship in the cell church takes little children and seeks to help them become mature disciples. Taking responsibility for a cell group provides a wonderful framework for a disciple-maker to minister to others while maturing in the faith. Giving birth to a new cell group provides new discipleship challenges, new skills, and fulfills the vision of Jesus to make disciples of all nations. Some will take Christ's commission to a new level and will become church planters and missionaries in other parts of the world.

Six
CELL GROUP MYTHS AND TRUTHS

Dear Robert Lay,

I am quite impressed by your ministry in Brazil and how you have spear-headed the resourcing of Brazil's growing cell church movement. It seems that the cell vision has deep roots in your country and that you and your team have worked hard to develop those roots. What do you think is the most basic reason for these established roots? What is the central message that has established this vision in the churches of Brazil?

Thanks for Your Time,

Pastor Jason

Dear Pastor Jason,

Let me respond with one core belief that has established the cell vision in Brazil: the cell is the church.

The cell is not an add-on. It is not a choice among many different ministries. It is not an inferior group that sits in the shadows of the real church. It is the church.

I can state this with complete confidence and establish this belief in our churches not because it's a good strategy, but because Jesus is the model for the church. He taught about the good news of the kingdom of God, a new life style here and now. He taught his church how to follow him, how to forego their professions and learn from him. To fishermen, he said, "Stop catching fish, I will show you how to catch the real fish, the most important and priceless ones. I will teach you and show you how to heal, cast out demons, provide comfort and demonstrate love."

His strategy was to relate to people where they lived. He taught his cell of disciples to meet the needs of the people in homes and on the street. Jesus was always out with the people, often on the road. On the road he met Zacchaeus, the blind, the lame, the sick, and all those with needs. His ministry did not have an address, an office, a classroom, or buildings.

His cell was a combat unit to engage the enemy on the front lines. It is the ecclesia, the church, on the move. His cell, which was church, was not engaged in a virtual war. His church was relational, not institutional. It dealt with real life and ground-level issues. As Bill Beckham says, "The cell is a mean, lean, fighting machine."

Jesus also provides us the right structure of the church. He organized it in groups of 3, 12, 70, and 120. Every one of these units had specific tasks to perform. Jesus was a great strategist, and gave us the right model.

So we can conclude that the cell is as much the church as the celebration. It is the body of Christ today, to fulfill his task of spreading the good news of the kingdom to all nations. Cells are his feet, his hands, and his eyes that minister to the needy, the poor, the prisoner, and the sick. The cell is the new wineskin designed by Jesus. If we want to keep the new wine, the gospel of free salvation, we better use the proper wineskin to contain it.

I pray that you will catch the vision for cell life and allow it to flow through your church.

May God richly bless you,

Robert Lay,
Pastor and mobilizer of the cell movement in Brazil

Myth:

Cells are an Extension of the Sunday Service

When I first researched cell churches I viewed cells as extensions of the true church that met on Sunday morning. I believed back then that the cells were simply a means to make the true church grow. Like many pastors, I viewed the celebration service as the real church.

Sunday morning church is the norm in western societies, not only because of the Protestant heritage but because people don't have time for more than one service. Many Sunday-oriented churches will emphasize small groups, but in reality, small groups are just one of the many programs. They are viewed as an optional-extra, not an essential. A person is free to join a small group or a ministry in the church. All activity is equally emphasized in order to keep Sunday services functioning well. Small groups are just a way to keep people coming back.

Truth:

The Cell Is the Church

The most common meeting place of the early church was the house. When we read the epistles, over and over we see the church in the house. Here are some examples:

- Romans 16:3-5: Greet Priscilla and Aquila, my fellow workers in Christ Jesus. They risked their lives for me.

Not only I but all the churches of the gentiles are grateful to them. Greet also the church that meets at their house.
- 1 Corinthians 16:19: The churches in the province of Asia send you greetings. Aquila and Priscilla greet you warmly in the Lord, and so does the church that meets at their house.
- Colossians 4:15: Give my greetings to the brothers at Laodicea, and to Nympha and the church in her house.
- Philemon 2: Apphia our sister, to Archippus our fellow soldier and to the church that meets in your home.

Most of the New Testament letters were written to first-century house churches. When Paul, for example, wrote about believers serving each other and waiting on each other during the Lord's supper, picture the context of the home. When Paul expounds on the operation of Spiritual gifts, envision a house church environment. When he highlights the role of each member in the body of Christ, imagine the warm atmosphere of the early house church. John Mallison writes, "It is almost certain that every mention of a local church or meeting, whether for worship or fellowship, is in actual fact a reference to a church meeting in a house."[11] Hadaway, S. Wright and DuBose add, "From the beginning, homes appeared to be the place for the most enduring dimensions of early church life." [12]

The house churches would come together for celebrations when possible. In 1 Corinthians, Paul writes to the city church of Corinth (verse 2), but then in chapter 16:19, he writes to the church in the house of Aquila and Priscilla.

The New Testament never defines the church in terms of buildings, preachers, or place. It defines the church in a very simple way. In my book, *Planting Churches that Reproduce*, I dedicate one chapter to the definition of the "church." After examining the evidence, I believe there are four simple principles that define what a church is:

First, the church should have more than three people as mentioned in Matthew 18:15-35.

Second, those in the church should be accountable to God-appointed leadership. This implies that the leaders will know the members and the members will have a relationship with the leaders. Hebrews 13:17 is clear, "Obey your leaders and submit to their authority. They keep watch over you as men who must give an account. Obey them so that their work will be a joy, not a burden, for that would be of no advantage to you." Being accountable to leadership requires commitment to the church (1 Corinthians 5; Galatians 6:1-2).

Third, scriptures make it clear that a church needs to operate under the lordship of Christ. As Lord, Jesus Christ is savior of the church. The church serves Christ. Christ died and rose so that he would be Lord of both the living and the dead. An assembly of people is not a true church unless Jesus is Lord.

Fourth, churches should participate in the sacraments of both baptism and the Lord's Supper (see Matthew 28:18-20; 1 Corinthians 11).

When my home group comes together, it's fully the church. We have God-appointed leadership, we meet regularly, we read God's word, and we participate in the sacraments—at times in the home group and at other times when all the home groups meet together for a common celebration. We are under the lordship of Christ and accountable to one another. It's a very simple gathering—simple and reproducible.

Myth:

Cells Should Encompass All Small Groups

In the book, *The Seven Deadly Sins of Small Group Ministry*, Robinson and Donahue say that it is a sin to define a small group too narrowly. According to the authors, all small groups should be given equal treatment, whether it is a group of ushers, deacons, normal cell group, or prison ministry group.

Ted Haggard wrote a book called *Dog Training, Fly Fishing, and Sharing Christ in the 21st Century*, in which he states that cell groups are far too limiting and need to be reinterpreted to fit a more open mindset.

These are just two examples of those who teach that small groups or cells are whatever you want them to be.

Some churches take the liberty for groups to meet once per month, break up at the end of the semester, or close during certain periods. Should all groups be considered cell groups?

Truth:

Start with a Quality Cell Definition

Like the early house churches, modern day cell churches believe the cell is the church and deserves a quality definition. From my research of growing cell churches around the world, I've derived the following definition:

Cells are groups of three to fifteen people who meet weekly outside the church building for the purpose of evangelism, community, and spiritual growth with the goal of making disciples who make disciples, which results in the multiplication of the cell.

Multiplication simply gives the context for a disciple to minister. Big Bear Christian Center defines their cell groups in a similar way but with a different emphasis:

> At the core of Big Bear Christian Center are life groups of three to fifteen people that meet weekly throughout Big Bear Bear Valley. Empowered by the Holy Spirit through prayer, their purpose is to make disciples through spiritual growth, community, and evangelism, resulting in group multiplication.

Cells have a lot of liberty with regard to where they will meet, the lesson they will follow, their homogeneity, level of participation, and what they call themselves. However, since the cell is the church, it is essential that cells maintain a high level of quality.

Cells must maintain a fine balance between flexibility (e.g., location, name, homogeneity, lesson, participation, etc.) and quality (e.g., clear definition).

Diminishing the quality of the cell will eventually cause the entire cell church strategy to crumble and eventually disintegrate.

Many have criticized the requirement that cells meet weekly. Why not meet every so often? Jim Egli and Dwight Marble's 2011 book, *Small Groups, Big Impact*, discovered key reasons for weekly cell meetings. The authors surveyed over three thousand small group leaders in twenty-one countries using a survey instrument and interviews to discover the right things that groups should do to be effective evangelists. One of the factors was the necessity for small groups to meet weekly.

They wanted to know whether it makes a difference how often a small group meets. The research revealed that it makes a tremendous difference. Groups that meet weekly experience dramatically more health and growth than groups that meet every other week. The authors write,

> Basically, we found that not much happens in a group using an every other week format. Why? Again the research tells us what but not why. However, having been involved in small groups for over 25 years, we don't think it's difficult to figure out. The main problem with an every-other-week group is that most people cannot make it to every meeting. Schedule conflicts, illness, family commitments, school programs and work projects keep almost everyone from making it to every meeting. Let's say that the average person misses small group once a month or so. If you and I are in the same group and you miss the first meeting this month and I miss the next, we might only see each other every sixth week or so. Meeting every other week makes it very hard to form close and meaningful relationships. If you are currently in a group that meets every other week, you might want to reevaluate with the group whether you want to begin meeting every week or at least three times a month. Another alternative is to supplement your every other week meetings with an additional monthly meeting that is geared to fun and outreach. If you are starting a new group, we recommend that you plan for your group to meet weekly, realizing that you should vary the format of your meetings so that you are consistently planning events such as parties, cookouts, and mission or ministry outreaches into your mix of activities.[13]

Defining a cell with a quality definition will help assure (not guarantee) that the members have a quality experience. Each part of a healthy definition must contribute to the truth that the cell is the church. Some people will come to the cell before they will ever attend a celebration service (gathering of the cells in one place). These cell-only members need to experience the true church of Jesus Christ.

Myth:

All Groups Must be Homogeneous

In 1998 the International Charismatic Mission in Bogota, Colombia found success in converting their cells into distinct categories of men, women, youth, and children. This categorization gave ICM a new vitality and growth. The church began to teach their network churches that this change was the "new model," the new path for all network churches to follow.

They promoted this new idea as the secret of their success. Family cells were out; strict homogenous categories were in.

Some churches accepted this new "homogeneous way" as the *only* way to do cell ministry. They believed that this was the new way to grow their churches and unconditionally accepted this model. They also pushed this new format as the new wave for all cell churches to use—that is, if the church wanted to grow and prosper.

Truth:

Allow Homogeneity to Naturally Develop as Cells Multiply

When a church finds something that works, it often promotes this to others as the new key or the way to become successful. It's so easy to desert the principles in favor of a new technique.

However, homogeneity should not be the primary focus. Rather, it should flow naturally as the need arises. I tell churches to first start with a clear cell definition to assure the quality of the group. After establishing a clear definition for all groups, homogeneity should be allowed to flow naturally.

I have a special affinity to family cells because the family is the foundation of society and in desperate need of healing today. Many cells allow children to be present in order to underscore the fact that the church of Jesus Christ is indeed a family.

The family group, however, is not the only way to organize cell ministry. Let's say there is a single person in a family cell group who overcame a drug addiction and is burdened to reach drug addicts. This person decides he wants to start a homogeneous cell group geared toward drug addicts. He completes the training, talks to his cell leader, and then launches out to lead a group of people who have struggled or are struggling with drugs. This would be a homogenous cell group focused on people with drug addiction.

Sometimes it's easier to reach people who have the same focus. Jane, for example, is a single adult and works fulltime. Jane has unchurched friends who are also single and work as professionals. Yes, Jane could invite them to the family cell, but she has always wanted to start her own cell group and has already completed the training. She launches a new cell group oriented toward adult professionals.

The new group is a very natural response to Jane's circle of influence. The entire church doesn't have to follow her example and divide into men's groups or women's groups to accommodate people like Jane. New homogeneous groups can spring forth naturally as the need arises.

Most cells in Jane's church are family oriented. Jane's church believes the family is the foundation of society and a society will live or die based on the health of the family unit. Yet, the church also practices the liberty of allowing new cells to form based on specific homogeneity.

Recently I led a men's cell and my wife leads a women's cell. Yet, my wife and I have primarily led family cells together in the past, especially with our children in the cell. When our children started a youth cell on a different night, we continued to lead an adult cell. Eventually, we felt led to multiply into a men's group and a women's group.

Myth:

One Person Should Be the Designated Host

Some cell ministries are convinced that a cell group should have a permanent host, and that the host should not be the cell leader.

There are many benefits to this view. First, it takes the burden off the cell leader to prepare for the cell meeting and handle all the duties of a host. It also allows someone else within the cell to take on a major responsibility.

The Elim Church, for example, strongly emphasizes the important ministry of the host family. Usually the host of each cell in the Elim Church is different from the actual cell leader.

The ministry of the host or hostess is essential for the successful growth of the cell group. But should each cell have a permanent host and should that host be different than the cell leader?

Truth:

A Shared Hosting Arrangement Is Often the Best Option

Some believers are naturally hospitable. They love to open their home to others. Others struggle with it. A regular rotation schedule can help share the burden and make cell ministry more doable. Rotating the meeting place also helps cell members realize that there is both blessings and responsibility in leading a cell group. Much can be learned about each other from meeting in different homes.

Regular rotation can also thrust the cell into the homes of those who have non-Christian friends who would not go to another person's home.

Yet, others insist that cells must rotate each week! I don't think it's necessary to rotate each week, but it's a great idea to rotate occasionally.

Myth:

Asking Everyone to Be in a Cell Stifles the Use of Spiritual Gifts

Some people have reacted to the idea that everyone should be in a cell group. "Wouldn't this stifle creativity and a person's giftedness?" they say. "Isn't it better if some join a cell while others join a particular program in the church?"

Many pastors believe that if someone has an urge to do something, he or she should start a new program. Or perhaps there's already a program operating in the church that will compliment that gifting. If not, the church should create a new ministry for the person. Is this how the early church operated?

Truth:

The Cell Group is the Best Place to Discover Spiritual Gifts

Earlier on in my cell ministry, a person tried to convince me to add additional programs so that people could find and exercise their spiritual gifts. "But in the small groups they'll have a chance to exercise their gifts," I countered. "Those with the gift of mercy will have the opportunity to minister to those in need—both in and outside the group. The person with the gift of teaching can clarify a passage of scripture. Those with the gifts of service or helps will have plenty of chances to use their gifts in the cell."

He didn't really hear what I was saying and our conversation that night ended in a stalemate. We both had strong opinions. But the conversation was a blessing in disguise because it forced me to revisit the issue of spiritual gifts and cell groups. The conversation stirred me to go back to scripture for answers.

When Paul wrote about the gift passages, he was writing to believers meeting in home groups (Ephesians 4; Romans 12 and 1 Corinthians 12-14). In all three passages about the gifts, he connects giftedness with the body of Christ. The only way to know where a person fits in the body of Christ is to discover his or her giftedness. The home atmosphere of the early church gave each person ample opportunity to test, prove and discover their own spiritual giftedness and place in the body of Christ.

I encourage cell leaders to study the gifts of the Spirit and to approach cell members about their gifts. One thing I discovered when writing the book, *The Spirit-Filled Small Group: Leading Your Group to Experience the Spiritual Gifts*, was that when a person knows and uses his or her spiritual gift, he or she will feel more responsible and needed. The person doesn't want to miss the cell, knowing that he or she is needed in the body of Christ.

I believe that today, more than ever, we need to get back to the small group as the primary place to exercise spiritual gifts. It is the most natural context to find, discover, and use spiritual gifts.

Seven
COMMUNITY MYTHS AND TRUTHS

Dear Dr. Cordle,

Community is so central to cell church life. But it seems like community is a huge challenge, especially in the West. From your years of working with cell groups, can you provide some insight in how community really works in cells?

Thanks for your time,

Pastor Mike

Dear Pastor Mike,

As you start off on your cell church journey, let me share a few thoughts with you about the kind of communities you will be creating.

A cell group is essentially a network of relationships. However, don't make the mistake of promoting cells primarily on the basis of community. When trying to convince someone to join a cell, it will not help to say something like, "In a cell you will find true community—deep, intimate relationships."

While it is true that we are made for community, remember that many people today both long for and fear close relationships. They have a God-given need for relationships with others, so there is a level of hunger for it. But they also fear true community. Maybe it is because they have rarely, if ever, experienced it. Families are often fractured today, and an increasing percentage of people don't know how to develop and maintain healthy relationships. So to try to entice them to a group with the promise of close community is like inviting them to an experience one of their greatest fears.

So as you bring people together in the community of a cell, realize many will not know how to relate. They will hide behind masks, be unreliable in commitment, and leave others' needs unmet. They may even offend each other. Community will be messy, but that doesn't mean it is failing. In fact, it is often in the mess that people grow the most.

For example, when the personality of one member irritates another, it is an opportunity to grow in love and patience. The irritated party's natural response may be to drop out or to look for another group that has people more like himself. But the Lord will want to help that person grow in love by accepting and forbearing with another.

If you say "Come to cell group, it is where you can meet

your needs for community," some may say "I don't need any more community. I have enough friends and family." (This is particularly true in rural areas.)

Community is a vital part of the cell group experience, but a healthy group is actually community with a cause. The cell has a purpose beyond itself. Even the person who has enough friends needs to grow to become like Christ and join his mission in the world. And the best way to do that is in community with other Christ-followers. A cell group is a group of people who are focused not just on each other, but on living out the purposes of God together. Following Jesus in community transforms us when it is externally focused.

A group that focuses only on those in the group will lose the outward focus which brings life. An ingrown group becomes stale, because it doesn't get the energy that comes from welcoming new people joining or serving the world. The experience of community is enhanced as the group gives out.

If you want to develop groups that experience deep community, teach them these principles from the beginning. At first, some won't believe you because it is so counter-intuitive. But when they practice this reality, they will go deeper and demonstrate the reality of true community for others.

Many blessings to you as you experience community,

Dr. Steve Cordle, Lead Ppastor of Crossroads, a growing cell church in Pittsburgh and author of <u>The Church in Many Houses.</u>

Myth:

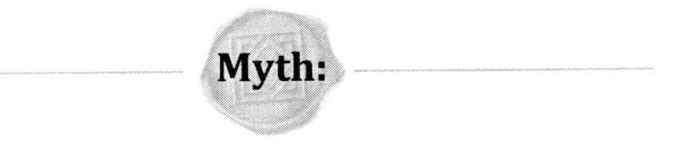

Cells Are Only about Community

Some believe that the primary reason for the cell group is community. I understand this myth because I live in the West and see firsthand how people are crying out for relationships and family. Children are raised in an environment of loneliness and separation. Their parents are divorced, and they feel ill equipped to establish long-term relationships. With this background, it's quite logical to emphasize the community aspect of small group ministry because it seems the most important. But is community the only reason we do cells?

Truth:

Cells Emphasize Community, Evangelism and Multiplication

Community is only one of the characteristics of effective cell groups. Cells also emphasize evangelism, spiritual growth, and leadership development which leads to multiplication.

A common error is to focus on one cell characteristic to the neglect of others. Cells, for example, need evangelism to carry community forward. Community can stagnate and dry-up without the vision for outreach. Evangelism, in fact, strengthens cell community by forcing its members to look beyond themselves and share the experience of community with others as a team.

Community is enhanced when given a common direction. Friendship among soldiers is forged in battle. They depend on each other and share their lives in a deep way. Cell members also grow closer when they go beyond their own concerns and reach out to those without Jesus.

Community given away through multiplying a prepared disciple continues Christ's concern for a lost world.

One of the great dangers of community is when it grows inward, stagnates, and the result is something far less than real community. Small groups without a pressure valve of outreach and vision beyond themselves can become self-absorbing. They need an outward thrust that will help them reach the next level of maturity.

I remember one cell group in Ecuador that focused entirely on community and refused to accept our new vision of community and evangelism. We discovered that this group had become one of the chief sources of gossip in the church. We tried to turn them around and to look outward, but they refused. Rather than a blessing, the group became a hindrance.

Stuart Gramenz, a church planter in Australia, teaches cell members the need for JOY (Jesus, Others, You). He tells them that they must first listen to Jesus. Only Jesus can transform hearts and minds.

Stuart explains that our human tendency is to want others to focus on us. Our sinful nature demands attention. Yet, true joy proceeds from Jesus to the needs of others.

Lastly, it's you. It seems logical to think of self after Jesus—my need for community. Yet, it's much more blessed to give than to receive. As we give out to others, we benefit much more.

Effective cell groups attempt to move each member from an emphasis on *me* to an emphasis on others. Others might be those in the group, or others might be those who have not yet become part of the group. Others might live in the neighborhood or are friends at work.

Myth:

The Cell Meeting Will Meet All the Needs

I watched a documentary about Lewis and Clark and their journeys into the great unknown. Before leaving, they were given a particular medicine that was described as the "cure-all potion." Whenever someone reported sickness or physical problems, they gave him this particular medicine. According to the medical records of that time period, it basically cleared out the system, but didn't actually help medically. Perhaps the psychological comfort was its main virtue.

Some in the cell movement highlight the ninety-minute cell meeting as the cure-all, a magical potion. It's supposed to meet all of the needs of the members.

The cell meeting is a powerful time, and God uses each member to heal others. Yet, it's only ninety minutes. The cell group meeting is essential. Yet, is it possible to expect too much from it?

Truth:

The Cell Meeting Is Only One Aspect of Community Life

Life is lived 24/7, whereas the cell meeting is for ninety minutes. Expecting the group meeting to take care of all of the spiritual transformation that group members need is absurd. But that's what many expect. I've found that while the group meeting is crucial, most of the significant growth is done outside of the ninety-minute time slot.

The cell group is a launching point for life lived between meetings. I tell those in my men's cell to pray for one another during the week. When we see each other on Sunday we ask about those requests. Yet, each member has to work out his Christian life each day of the week.

I get excited when cell members stay in touch through texting, email, phone calls, or personal meetings. A phone call from another member can go a long way. The cell plays an important role in bringing believers together, but it is only a part of that process.

Rob Hastings, the new lead pastor at Big Bear Christian Center, writes:

> Recently, I have been trying to understand what community is, and how we can experience it in our cells. I am beginning to see that perhaps I am not supposed to make community happen only in my group, but make sure that everyone in my group is living in close relationship. I have come to realize that I cannot "facilitate" community within our 1.5 hour meeting. I want people to meet together outside the meeting, encourage each other, and attempt to create community during the week.

Rob realized that the cell couldn't meet all the community and personal needs of the group members. The cell meeting was limited in its scope and purpose.

Both cell and celebration are important in the life of each believer but neither completes God's purpose. They point us in the right direction and play a critical role in our lives. They function like spring boards that propel us forward in our daily lives.

Myth:

The Cell Leader Should Develop All the Relationships in the Group

One particular cell leader at Brookside Free Methodist Church was troubled with the time requirements of cell ministry—specifically with the building of relationships. With a full-time job, a young family, and very little time to offer the church and the cell, he thought he was supposed to also develop the relationships between the cell members.

Many cell leaders are burdened with cell leadership because they think they are responsible to make community happen in the cell. Is this true?

Truth:

People within the Group Should Share the Relational Load

I told the leader at the Free Methodist church that he didn't need to take the community burden upon himself and that it wasn't his role. I told him that each member of the cell is responsible to build relationships with each other. I told him that his task was to direct the body of Christ (e.g., those in the cell) to love and serve one another.

Relationship building is such an essential part of cell ministry that it should not be a one-person responsibility. All members must be involved.

Scripture tells us that we are all ministers, all priests of the living God (Revelation 1:6). The Bible tells us in

1 Corinthians 12 that each plays a vital role in the body of Christ. Ephesians 4:16 says, "From him the whole body, joined and held together by every supporting ligament, grows and builds itself up in love, as each part does its work."

A true cell group is about everyone in it. If the leader is the one who does everything, the members will not learn the importance of reaching out to one another. They will not grow together. Robert Lay, the leader of an exciting cell resourcing movement in Brazil, repeats this phrase over and over: "every house a church and every member a minister."

We are all ministers. The cell is uniquely positioned to make this truth a reality. Everyone should be involved in making it work.

One way to encourage members to reach out is to meet together during the week in gender specific groups. The Methodists popularized these smaller sub-groups which they called "bands." The Methodists were famous for their classes (cells), yet the bands were also part of the Methodist make-up. These bands were sub-groups of the class meetings and met for deeper relationships and accountability. When they met together they would ask the following questions:

1. What known sins have you committed since our last meeting?
2. What temptations have you met with?
3. How were you delivered?
4. What have you thought, said, or done, of which you doubt whether it be sin or not?
5. Have you nothing you desire to keep secret?

The cell leader should encourage members to meet in smaller sub-groups for ministry, play sports together, pray over the telephone, or any other activity that encourages loving relationships.

When the leader assumes responsibility for all the relational building, he or she is taking on an unnecessary burden. It's not the one Jesus gives. Jesus said in Matthew 11:28-30, "Come to me, all you who are weary and burdened, and I will give you rest. Take my yoke upon you and learn from me, for I am gentle and humble in heart, and you will find rest for your souls. For my yoke is easy and my burden is light."

Eight
EVANGELISM MYTHS AND TRUTHS

Dear Mr. Neighbour,

You grew up in the home of one of the cell church pioneers. Your father always speaks with great passion for evangelism and this same passion seems to be woven through you. Would you mind sharing with me about how evangelism really works in cells?

I really appreciate whatever you have time to share.

Pastor Carlos

Dear Pastor Carlos,

Reaching people for Christ through cell groups is a whole new way of life for most western Christians. They usually define "evangelism" as sharing a two-minute testimony about their conversion experience with a stranger in hopes that God will send a lightning bolt of conviction on the unsuspecting soul. The truth is, most western Christians don't have much significant interaction with unchurched people and rarely share their testimony. They've embedded themselves in a religious subculture that shields them from social interaction with the outside world.

Conversely, in a healthy biblical community such as a cell group, there are no strangers. One's testimony is shared through a deep friendship and lifestyle. Good times are celebrated and bad times are endured together. Life is lived out in the midst of relationships with people who are both near and far away from Christ.

As I reflect on my personal experiences with group-based relational evangelism, it's usually a quiet conversion experience for the new believer. The person first becomes a friend of a member of the group well before making a commitment to Christ. Sometimes they come to cell meetings and other times they shy away from formal gatherings, but they are still a part of our group. Time and time again, I have visited with new believers who say, "Hey, I almost forgot to tell you! Saturday morning I woke up and realized I needed to give everything to God. I thanked him for sending his Son, and I think I'm finally connecting with God."

The first time this "sneaking into the kingdom through the side door" happened, I was taken aback. After all, I did all that hard work and I didn't even get to pray "the sinner's prayer" with the person!

God began to give me and my co-leaders a new perspective on evangelism. He showed us that we were called to serve unbelievers and not talk them into becoming like us. Our job was to become genuine friends—friends who revealed our weaknesses and insecurities, shared life experiences both good and bad, and loved one another unconditionally and without expectation. When this kind of friendship started developing, the unbelievers in our group's web of relationships served with us, laughed with us, and even cried with us.

As you experience cell group evangelism, keep in mind that it's about loving people enough to become a real friend so they can see Christ in you! Come to think of it, a two-minute testimony is good to have in case you need it when the Spirit prompts you to share with a stranger, but you'll need a two-hour testimony when a close friend wants to know why you believe the Christian message.

Many blessings,

Randall Neighbour,
president of Touch Outreach and author
of various books on cell ministry.

Myth:

The Focus of the Cell is Entirely Evangelistic

Growing cell churches around the world have learned to do cell evangelism well. Their cells not only engage in fellowship but also evangelistic outreach. One of the key differences, in fact, between cells and small groups in general, is an evangelistic emphasis. Cell churches position their cells to evangelize and multiply, while many conventional churches primarily focus on community and fellowship in the small groups. Yet is it possible to focus too much on cell evangelism?

Truth:

Effective Cells Need a Strong Core of Believers

While cells should reach out to unbelievers, the only way to multiply is to have a core of believers who are going through training and preparing to reproduce themselves.

Ken Brown, a cell church planter in Delaware, already had a red-hot passion to reach unbelievers through cell ministry, but he discovered that establishing a core was the best way to do this. However, I asked him to write a blog about what he discovered:

> I long to see the cells become a hotbed of evangelistic activity that will infuse our cell system with zealous new believers, growing and developing until they take their place in ministry for the kingdom. So, after finishing Joel's

book, *Passion and Persistence*, I asked myself, "What can I do to create an atmosphere in my cell where this Spirit-born drive can be expressed by all of the members?"

As I reviewed what I had read, I realized that Elim's requirement of a second cell meeting per week was a great way to prioritize evangelism in the busy lives of my cell members. So, in our next Sunday evening cell meeting I asked those who were willing to meet with me briefly on Thursday evening to plan the next cell meeting. We divided the four parts of the cell among those present, encouraged each other to complete the training track, and most importantly, decided who we were going to invite to the cell from among our unsaved friends and family. The scheduling of this meeting of my core became a filter that allowed those really interested in winning others to express it by attending. The following cell meeting was attended by two who had not met Jesus and who, although they did not respond, at least heard the good news.

Ken realized that he needed to mobilize the core believers into a team to effectively evangelize.

He learned this from the Elim Church, which has two separate meetings—one for the core of believers to plan and pray and the other is the normal evangelistically-oriented cell group.

The normal cell at Elim meets on Saturday night. The planning team meets on Thursday (or Wednesday) night to plan for the normal evangelistic cell group.

Anyone who is a believer in Jesus Christ can participate in the mid-week planning meeting. The planning meeting allows those with a hunger to serve Jesus Christ to become more deeply in cell life, being able to plan, pray, and act. Those who participate in the mid-week planning meeting are considered the cell nucleus or core. Elim realizes that the best cells are led by teams, rather than one individual, and the mid-week planning meeting provides the setting for team involvement to happen. René Molina, senior pastor of Elim Los Angeles, said to me, "The planning meeting is the opportunity for members to show their concern to reach more lost people. They come together because they have zeal to see something more happen in their cell. It's also an opportunity to see how committed people are."

Elim Church is convinced that the success of the cell group depends on the nucleus, or team. Elim has learned from experience not to exalt one person. They truly believe that success in cell ministry means training an army of leaders. Mario Vega said, "The preparation of the nucleus is part of the culture of Elim. After sixteen years, the cell members know that the goal of the cell is multiplication and they prepare to make it happen."

Remember that Jesus also had a team of three within his group of twelve. Michael Mack has written an excellent book called *Burnout-Free Small Group Leadership*. Mack argues against the Lone Ranger leader and expounds the benefits of the leadership team. Jesus developed his team, as did Paul. Ecclesiastes 4:12 says, "Though one may be overpowered, two can defend themselves. A cord of three strands is not quickly broken."

Myth:

Evangelism in the Cell Church Is Only Relational

I coached one pastor who was very well versed in cell church teaching. He asked me to coach him to make sure he was on the right track.

He understood from books and seminars that the only correct way to evangelize in the cell church was through relationships. He had read critical comments about all other methods of evangelism that weren't relational, and he wanted to make sure his cell church followed the pure cell philosophy. He supposed he needed to make friends with people who did not know Jesus and over a long period of time win them for Christ.

He had cultivated a few strong relationships with non-Christians and had even taken one of the prospects on a camping trip. He was now waiting for that fruit to produce. Yet, he also knew that he needed to reach a lot of new people to keep his church plant thriving. He really didn't know what to do.

Truth:

Don't Limit Yourself to One Evangelistic Method

I told this particular church planting pastor to throw open the doors to new evangelistic possibilities. He didn't need to focus only on relational outreach. He had a clear burden for providing food and clothing for the hungry. As he prayed about the possibilities, he established a pantry in the midst of his small town in Texas and began to win the hearts and minds of those in the town through meeting their physical needs. Cell ministry was his main philosophy of ministry, and he mobilized cell members to help in the pantry, share the gospel, and follow-up with those interested.

Scripture tells us to plant and water and that God will give the increase. It doesn't mention one particular way to evangelize. Jesus evangelized through open air preaching, one-on-one relationships, and healing people.

Cell churches also use a wide variety of outreach events. Many cell churches have church wide harvest events, in which cell members invite the unchurched to an evangelistic- oriented event. Some cells reach out through neighborhood evangelism, picnics, feeding the hungry, prayer walking, and outreach events.

Relational evangelism works best in conjunction with other forms of outreach. It's unwise to only rely on getting to know a few friends over a long period of time when the rest of the non-Christians are going to hell without Jesus.

Although I promote many types of evangelistic outreach, I'm not in favor of establishing evangelistic programs that compete with the cell. Such programs require a lot of work and manpower to keep them going, and eventually take away the personal outreach time of the cell members.

I'm simply saying that cell members, cell leaders, and pastors should do everything possible to reach those who don't know Jesus. My daughter is a youth cell leader. She asked me to use my car to drive around the youth cell members to pass out hamburgers and to evangelize the poor and needy of Moreno Valley. We bought hamburgers from McDonalds and passed them out to homeless people, while sharing the good news. Everyone in the van was praying and asking God for direction concerning who to meet, where to turn the car, and what to say to those who received the hamburgers. God opened up all kinds of doors, and we shared Jesus with a lot of people.

Because people are so different, we need many ways to reach them. Some will come to Christ one way and others will respond in a different manner. All ways are important for the furtherance of the gospel. God might stir up cell members to pray for the sick, feed the hungry, or pass out evangelistic fliers. If we're only sowing the seed with one or two people, our harvest will be slim. I tell people to try every means possible to evangelize.

Myth:

A Cell Group Must Add a Certain Number of New Christians before It Can Multiply

I've always been impressed with how the Yoido Full Gospel Church (Pastor David Cho) asks each cell to win two people to Jesus each year. Those leaders who don't reach their goal go to Pray Mountain to fast and pray for unbelieving hearts to soften. I often joke about these leaders being "sent to Prayer Mountain" as a "disciplinary action." From what I understand of Cho's church, cells are only encouraged to win two people. They are not *required* to do so.

I know of another church in the U.S. who made a church-wide rule that each cell had to win three people to Jesus or the cell could not multiply. In other words, if the cell won two people to Jesus, they weren't allowed to give birth to a new cell until one more received Jesus.

This pastor was passionate about evangelism, and he was very effective at it. He would often ask unchurched people to hang out with him, and he encouraged the church to have the same passion. He rightly realized that evangelism had to be at the center of cell ministry, and that it wasn't wise to multiply a cell that had not engaged in evangelism.

This pastor influenced other churches to make a similar rule. I spoke at one of those churches a few years back. They repeated to me their new vision of not multiplying unless the cell brought three people to Jesus. This particular church had a hard time winning people to Jesus in their particular community and the groups grew larger and larger. They wondered what they should do.

Truth:

Cell Members Should Evangelize but Avoid "Cell Rules"

We all rejoice when people come to Christ, and yes, the cells must evangelize. Yet, we have to be careful not to make legalistic rules that stifle creativity. Making such rules might seem like a great way to preserve quality, but rules don't produce life. Galatians 5:1 tells us, "It is for freedom that Christ has set us free. Stand firm, then, and do not let yourselves be burdened again by a yoke of slavery."

I do believe that every cell member should be involved in actively reaching out before multiplication occurs. Without such effort, the cell is not mature enough to multiply. Yet I think it's unwise to place a number of converts on the cell as a condition for multiplication.

I prefer to talk about each member exercising his or her muscles in evangelism, rather than a certain number saved for multiplication to occur. A future leader or member of a leadership team should have experience in actively evangelizing. If the leader fills the cell with people already in the church, the cell will reproduce an ingrown cell. Why? Because the leader and members have not learned to actively reach out.

If we believe the goal of the cell is to make disciples who make disciples, it's important that the potential disciples have been using their evangelistic muscles to reach out and win new people. The key is active evangelism. Again, like so many things, good intentions can become means of enslavement. A rule such as, "you must lead three people to Jesus" will quickly become a burden rather than a blessing and even slow down the process of multiplication.

Myth:

If the Cell Emphasizes Evangelism and Multiplication, It Won't Grow in Community

Many people resist the idea of evangelism and multiplication because they think community development will suffer. The assumption is that community and evangelism mix like water and oil. After all, how could a Christian share transparently if a non-Christian showed up one week or an unchurched person started attending? Wouldn't that prevent deep discussion? The common assumption is that community among group members must be the focus, and the only way to truly grow in that community is to have the same people present week after week.

Truth:

Evangelism that Leads to Multiplication Enhances the Community in the Group

Community comes to life when it has a purpose. When a group has a vision to reach out and penetrate a lost world for Jesus, people come together in a new way. Sharing community to the lonely and isolated keep the community fresh.

Ben Wong, founder of the Cell Church Mission Network, recently told me that the cells at Shepherd Community Church in Hong Kong don't always have a regular weekly cell meeting in a house, although the cells meet weekly. Rather, the cell meeting is often held on the streets, at a shopping center, or anywhere where they can reach those who don't know Jesus. The cell community grows as the cell members minister to others.

When a group looks inwardly, it shrivels and dies. If the main purpose is fellowship among members, it will stagnate. When the group reaches out, the community among members is strengthened.

Myth:

The Cell Leader Does the Evangelism

I've seen a lot of burdened cell leaders who condemn themselves for the lack of evangelistic growth in the group.

Perhaps the leader attends a seminar or reads a book about cell evangelism and then assumes he or she has to make it happen. The leader begins to feel like Atlas, the mythical figure who carried the world on his shoulders. Leading the cell becomes more of a chore than a delight.

Truth:

Each Member of the Cell Should be Involved in Outreach

The body of Christ is comprised of diverse members who build the body together. I've mentioned repeatedly that every member is a minister (Revelation 1:6).

Luke 5:1-7 is the story about Jesus and a great catch of fish. The disciples had fished all night and caught nothing. But at Jesus' command, they cast out their nets once again. We read in verses 6 and 7, "When they had done so, they caught such a large number of fish that their nets began to break. So they signaled their partners in the other boat to come and help them, and they came and filled both boats so full that they began to sink." Then in verse 10, it states that Simon and his partners, James and John, were astonished at the catch.

In the first reference to Peter's partners, a technical term for a business partner is used. But in verse 10, Luke uses a different Greek word for partners, one that means those who have koinonia fellowship. Peter and his partners worked together to haul in the huge catch. As they would work together to catch men, their fellowship would take on a new meaning. Likewise, in cell ministry, evangelism is a partnership. The idea of net fishing means that each person participates in evangelism and then the harvest is eventually reeled in through the participation of those taking care of the nets. Net fishing takes the burden off one person and places it on each person. It's a group effort and everyone is involved.

I was recently in a church in Puerto Rico that started in a cell and grew to twenty-four cells in three years. I interviewed leader after leader and discovered that each one of them was initially invited to the cell as a non-Christian (and often in bondage to addictions), born again in the cell, nurtured in the cell, and eventually discipled through the cell equipping process. The beauty of this church was that every person saw himself as a minister who needed to fish for lost souls. Nets in the form of cell groups were being thrown all over the city, and they were bringing in a large catch of fish.

I taught another seminar in the state of Washington that highlighted the net fishing feature of small group ministry with the clear message that the cells were boats in an ocean of lost men and women. I talked to a person in the church that Sunday who years earlier was ready to commit suicide because of frustration and depression in life. In the midst of his personal crisis, a cell member, an old-time high school friend, invited him to the cell group. Instead of committing suicide, he found life and liberty in Jesus Christ. God used a cell member to reach this person. The entire cell participated in discipling him. It was a team effort. One person invited, while others were equally as effective to serve and minister to this person and help him become a disciple of Jesus.

I tell people in my seminars that I can't reach the people they can reach. God has placed a certain number of people around each of us, and we are the best missionaries to those particular people.

If you're a cell leader reading this book, refuse to assume all the responsibility. Empower others. Make sure that evangelism is a group event.

Nine

MULTIPLICATION MYTHS AND TRUTHS

Dear Pastor Kniesel,

Cell church literature talks a lot about multiplication. In some cases, the writers make it sound like multiplication automatically happens at a rapid rate. I'd like to hear an honest perspective that describes how multiplication really happens. Would you mind sharing your point of view?

Thanks for your insight,

Pastor Dave

Dear Pastor Dave,

It is natural and desirable that every cell should multiply. Often I have heard that a cell should multiply every nine to twelve months. Yet, I have not met a church where this continuously is the case. As a matter of fact, observation and experience brought me to the realization that if on the average a cell multiplies every two to four years, it is doing great!

Many cell leaders and cell members have been put under extreme pressure to produce something which can only be achieved through growth and development. This cannot be forced by a predetermined timetable.

What factors are involved in the multiplication of a cell? The first important matter is the thorough preparation and training of the first and subsequent leaders. It is very common to train a cell leader by having him or her attend leadership classes. Yet the more important training is not the lectures on how a cell is being run, but the character of the future leader. This is not achieved through class lectures, but in daily living and by observing a mature leader over a longer period of time. The aim or vision of the cell is not only multiplication as far as numbers are concerned, but multiplication in lifestyle (living in the Spirit) and ministry (doing the work of service).

Multiplication further depends on the evangelism in the cell and the church. Where I live, in Europe, there is very limited acceptance to the gospel message. Yet we do see people come to Christ at a continuous rate, only the numbers are not as large as in many other countries. We need more time to pray for and reach out to people before we gain enough of their confidence that they are willing to hear the gospel.

Then multiplication depends also on whether the individual cell members are in a healthy process of discipleship. Of course, this will really never stop, yet there must be a solid foundation of growth in the believer.

As the cell is functioning, the cell leader is always on the lookout for a future leader. It is never too early to begin preparing a future cell leader. Do not wait until you must multiply. When you feel your growing cell should multiply, you should only do so if you have a prepared leader ready. Speak with your pastor to have his backing, set a date, and then speak with the cell members. Make sure that each member realizes that multiplication will actually strengthen the cell. It is an occasion for celebration.

Yes, have a vision for multiplication. Pray and work towards it. Encourage the cell to do the same. But don't think you are failing because you haven't multiplied in twelve months! As you keep the vision alive, you will reach multiplication!

May the Spirit empower you,

Werner Kniesel,
Lead Pastor emeritus of a strategic cell church in Zurich, Switzerland and author of various books.

Myth:

All Cells Must Multiply within Six Months

Earlier in the cell church movement (1990s) grandiose announcements were made concerning cell group multiplication. Some proclaimed that all cells should multiply after a certain time period.

And certainly, in some countries and cultures, the cells were multiplying at a very rapid rate. In my 1996 study of cell churches (chart below), I discovered that it only took four months to multiply a cell at the International Charismatic Mission in Bogota, Colombia.

Average Time To Multiply a Cell Group in Each Country	Colombia	18 weeks
	El Salvador	22 weeks
	Ecuador	24 weeks
	Peru	28 weeks
	Honduras	39 weeks
Average Length Of Time To Multiply Cell Group: 26 weeks (6 months)		

God brought revival to Colombia, and churches were growing at an amazing rate. We can rejoice in such rapid growth, but a lot depends on the receptivity of the country. For example, multiplication time frames in Turkey or Spain would be much slower. In such countries, the group would first need to evangelize, convert people, and disciple them. Someone would need to lead the new group. Is there a set time period for cells to multiply?

Truth:

Multiplication Rates Depend on Receptivity Levels

Raymond Ebbett was a missionary with the Christian and Missionary Alliance in Colombia for many years where he witnessed rapid growth. Then Raymond and his wife moved to Spain, where he found people resistant to the Gospel and church growth very slow.

Both countries spoke Spanish and both cultures had many similar traits. The receptivity of the people, however, was as different as night and day. Those in Spain took a long time to receive Christ, make it through the equipping, and even longer to become cell leaders.

Raymond learned a lot about soil and its place in reaping the cell harvest. He knew firsthand that the soil played a vital factor in the harvest. Some soil is hard and rocky. It takes a lot of plowing before growth can occur. Other soil has already been tilled and watered. It is ready to produce growth.

Raymond understands that cells don't grow and multiply in six months in Spain. He realizes that such a pronouncement would only discourage a cell leader and cause him or her to quit in despair.

One of my favorite cell churches is pastored by Werner Kniesel in Switzerland (see the introduction to this chapter). Werner's church has approximately two hundred fifty cells and is having a worldwide impact. I'll never forget one of the conversations I had with Werner while doing a seminar in his church. He told me that he had heard all the grand proclamations of a single rate of worldwide cell multiplication. Yet, he also knew the difference between Switzerland and other cultures.

Some countries are experiencing revival and multitudes are coming to know Jesus Christ. In these countries, cells readily reap the harvest, train new leaders, and multiply quickly—perhaps in six months. Other places are hard and difficult. It takes a long time to see conversions and even longer to prepare new leaders. Multiplication rates depend on prepared hearts.

Cell ministry can be very difficult in many places around the world. Few are coming to Jesus. Ministry is hard. Proclaiming that cells must multiply in a certain time period will probably hinder the natural progress of cell ministry.

The church in the Philippines is experiencing revival and church growth on an unprecedented scale. I hear glowing reports about rapid multiplication in that country. Churches are packed to overflowing. Cells are multiplying rapidly. People are giving themselves to the work of God and multiplying cells at a rapid pace. But this is an exception. In most places around the world, growth is much slower. It would be easy for a pastor ministering in the Philippines to expect multiplication to take place on the same scale everywhere in the world.

The United States is now in a post-Christian era and receptivity is much lower. Jeff Tunnell, senior pastor of Big Bear Christian Center, in Big Bear, California writes,

> On our journey in building cells and multiplying them, we have fallen into the trap of adopting someone else's rules for closing cells that do not multiply within a certain time frame. Hearing comments like, a baby can be born in nine months so surely we can multiply a cell in that amount of time, seemed to make sense at the time. But when faced with a sincere and healthy leader who has been shepherding people that move away, or have economy driven schedules with multiple jobs that do not fit into the cell meeting schedule, it becomes difficult to close the cell based on non-multiplication!

Frequency of multiplication must rest upon the health of the cell, its leader and an ability to sustain the multiplication. Many other good factors should exist beyond a simple timeframe such as, benchmarks of maturity, available supervisors/coaches, support systems in place, accountability to leadership, and new souls being won to Christ. Time alone has not been a good benchmark for multiplying cells. I agree with the attitude that if a cell has not multiplied in a certain time frame that we should examine why, spend time seeking God for insight and guidance to correct the weaknesses that may exist and regroup for the next season. Let's keep cells open and functioning for the right reasons.[14]

I applaud Jeff's quote here and wholeheartedly agree with it. There's a time and season when multiplication will take place, but it's best not to try and enforce impossible rules.

Myth:

Shut Down a Cell Group That Has Not Multiplied within One Year

Faith Community Baptist Church in Singapore popularized this approach back in the '90s. They insisted that if a cell did not multiply in one year, it was not healthy and therefore should not continue.

Following the Singapore philosophy, one pastor wrote, "Everything that has life has a cycle. As you study the cell, it must give life. If you keep a cell [open] that is not multiplying, it will die. The choice is life and death." This particular pastor gave their cells one year to multiply. If it didn't multiply in that time period, the church would shut down the cell.

Truth:

Keep Working with Cell Groups That Are Not Growing

I don't believe in shutting down cells for failure to multiply. It's hard enough for someone to multiply a cell without the added burden of "possible failure." While some can handle this kind of pressure, most will wilt under such demands.

The cell group leader is already pained and distressed when none of the invitees to the group show up. Demanding that the cell multiple or close is the final blow.

Granted, I do believe that cell closure is valid when and if the cell malfunctions. I've personally been involved in closing cells because of sin. In one case, the leader had an affair and failed to repent. We had to remove this person from leadership and train someone else to lead the cell.

Even in the human body, bad cells that divide can kill the entire body. A leader might fall into pornography, alcoholism, or false doctrine. Upper level leaders need to move in and replace the leader or close the group. But such decisions should stay within the upper circles of cell leadership.

While closure may be necessary at times, it should not be the norm. And certainly no cell should be closed before every possible avenue to multiply the group has been exhausted.

Myth:

A Cell Multiplies When It Reaches Fifteen People

This myth developed during the early years of cell multiplication. David Cho, the father of the modern day cell movement, taught that a group should grow to fifteen people and then half of them would start a new group. Most people assumed that this was the only way to multiply a group. Cho did it this way and so should everyone else.

In this approach, the cell leader was always looking for a number of people to join the group in order to multiply. When that particular number arrived, it was time to multiply. If the cell didn't grow to that point, multiplication was put on hold.

Truth:

Cells Multiply When a Disciple-Maker is Ready to Lead the New Group

New cells require new leaders. It's not the size of the group that determines multiplication; it's the readiness of new leadership. Waiting too long can stagnate and hinder the process, just like launching too early can do the same thing. Rather than focusing on leadership development, the old paradigm of multiplying at fifteen frequently became a dreaded goal.

A long time ago I operated under the mentality of automatic multiplication when the group reached fifteen. I tried my best to convince the groups under my care that it was for their own good that they multiplied at fifteen people.

One constant problem was trying to figure out when the group truly reached fifteen. Some weeks the group might have fifteen but other weeks, eight or less showed up. I also found that as the group came closer to the magical number of fifteen, some families would inevitably leave. They just didn't want to go through the pain of saying good-bye.

Over the years, cell churches have learned that focusing on a certain number within the group wasn't nearly as important as preparing the new leader to lead the next cell group. Trained leadership is the key behind cell ministry. As leaders are trained and sent forth, there's a new vision for multiplication.

While the potential leader is in the process of going through the training track, he or she is also involved in leading certain parts of the cell (e.g., worship, prayer, ice-breaker, vision casting).

Developing a God-honoring equpping track, therefore, is one of the most important goals in the cell church. Churches must develop strong equipping tracks that produce new leaders. Without equipping, cells don't have a way to move ahead.

An unequiped member of a cell will feel uncomfortable about becoming the next leader. Yet, an equipped member will understand the principles behind multiplication and will know how to lead the next group. Much of the fear will diminish after the potential leader has gone through the training.

One pastor recently questioned me about the importance of the equipping track. Was it really necessary? It sounded so programmatic to him. I shared with him that the equipping track was necessary because no one was going to lead a cell group who didn't feel equipped. New cell leaders will face enemy fire. They will need to draw on the training they received in the mother cell group and through the equipping process.

Those soldiers who came back alive from World War II commented over and over about how boot camp prepared them for the horrors to come. In the midst of battle, soldiers often responded subconsciously to what they had been taught in their training. They had repeated the drills so many times in training, they quickly responded when facing the enemy. Often the boot camp training made the difference between life and death

The boot camp for the new leader is the equipping track and the practical experience gained in the cell group. Both are essential to prepare new cell leaders.

So the goal of every cell church and cell group is to prepare a equipping track and then to get people through it. In my book, *Leadership Explosion*, I go into detail about what equipping tracks are and how to make them work in the cell church. Cell multiplication is all about developing disciples who make other disciples.

Myth:

When God Wants the Cell to Multiply It Will Do So Naturally

As a pastoral team in Ecuador, we determined our yearly cell goals based on those in the training track, and each of the network pastors were responsible for part of the yearly goal.

As we neared the time of reporting those goals, one of the pastor's network of cells wasn't doing very well. We were trying to encourage him, but he commented, "When God wants to multiply my cells, he will do so."

He was throwing everything on God and taking the responsibility off himself. And yes, in one sense, only God can do the work. Yet, where is the point in which such catch-phrases become excuses to hide behind?

Truth:

It's Best to Make Clear Plans for Multiplication

This pastor could have said, "I need to lower my goals," or "I am experiencing more problems than I realized," and we would have understood. Yet, by saying, "God will multiply the cells when he wants to," he was making a spiritual statement (playing the God card) that no one could dispute. It was like he was saying, "If you have a problem with what is happening in my network, go to God because he controls what's happening." End of discussion.

God is interested in multiplication. He's already told us to make disciples of all nations. Granted, we cannot manipulate God. We can't tell him when to do something or how to do it. His ways are mysterious. Yet, it does glorify him when we make clear plans to fulfill what is clearly stated in scripture.

A pregnant mother knows when she will give birth. She has nine months before the baby appears, whether she's ready or not. Wise mothers will prepare for the new birth, get the crib ready, buy new baby clothing, and obtain the proper medical care. Fruitful cell leaders follow a similar pattern.

They see the cell as the womb to produce new disciples who make other disciples. They look for FAST cell members (faithful, available, servant-hearted, and teachable), get them involved in the cell, and then make sure those members receive the church's training. In other words, they don't just hope multiplication will happen. They plan for it. Proverbs 21:5 says, "The plans of the diligent lead to profit as surely as haste leads to poverty." Clear planning is important. God wants us to plan and then prepare for multiplication. If no one is in the training track, the first goal is get them there. Future multiplication goals will be based on preparation through the cell and graduation from the training track.

Myth:

Multiplication Destroys the Relationships in the Group

Cell groups might resist multiplying for the fear of losing relationships with others in the group.

The word *division* is often associated with cell multiplication. Many feel that multiplication disrupts relationships, and they want to avoid it at all costs. Can anything be done to maintain relationships between multiplied cells?

Truth:

Relationships Can Be Maintained after Multiplication

The mother and daughter cell should plan social times to renew relationships. The mother cell leader or cell supervisor might connect individuals together between the two groups. And most cell churches have weekly celebration events. During the celebration services, the cell members can reconnect to maintain the close relationships.

One cell church in Honduras asked the mother and daughter cells to meet together for the first several months after multiplication. The mother and daughter cell would afterwards decide how often they wanted to meet.

When the mother cell leader coaches the daughter cell leader, there is a better chance to maintain close ties. Mother cell leaders make great coaches. They know their baby. They understand the new leader and his or her struggles. Multiplication leaders also have a vested interest in the success of the new group.

Ideally, therefore, it's best for the mother cell leader to coach the new cell. I used to teach that the mother cell leader was always the one who coached the daughter cell group, but I now only suggest this relationship. I realize that it's not always possible to connect the mother cell leader with the daughter leader (often for the lack of time).

I'd rather have a coach who is not the mother but who is faithful, available, servant-hearted, and teachable than have the mother cell leader coach the new cell without being able to commit the time necessary to see the daughter cell grow and prosper.

Even if the new daughter cell is assigned to another supervisor, there are various times and places for the mother and daughter cell to interact.

Ten
COACHING MYTHS AND TRUTHS

Dear Dr. Egli,

There are a lot of opinions about coaching. Some see it as being central, but others don't emphasize it because they can't seem to make it work. I'd like to know what your research and experience reveals about coaching and its importance to group life.

Thanks for your time,

Pastor Rob

Dear Pastor Rob,

During the late 1990s, I was a frustrated cell group consultant who was puzzled by why so many churches failed to get long-term success with small groups. I wanted to know why some churches had wonderful success with small groups, while other churches struggled.

I began to statistically analyze the differences between healthy, growing small group systems and struggling, stagnant ones. I discovered that Dwight Marable of Missions International was doing almost identical research. Dwight and I joined forces to discover through careful, extensive research how churches can have thriving small group systems. To date, we have surveyed over 3,000 small group leaders in more than 200 churches to find the answer to our questions.

Our research revealed that one factor matters more than any other. That most pivotal factor for long-term success in small group ministry is the proactive coaching of small group leaders.

What do we mean by that? Proactive coaching means that small group leaders have someone who is encouraging them, praying for them and helping them solve their problems.

The question is not, "Does your small group system have coaches?" Almost every church has some kind of supervisors assigned to oversee their small group leaders. The real question is, "Are the people assigned to oversee your small groups actively coaching their leaders?"

Our research revealed four actions that proactive coaches do:

1. They meet personally with their leaders to encourage them and help them grow as leaders.
2. They consistently pray for them.
3. They occasionally visit their small groups.
4. They get their leaders together so that they can learn from one another and minister to each other.

Churches with strong coaching carried out through these four behaviors have much stronger small group systems. Their leaders and groups are healthier and their groups see more people come to Christ, more people join their groups, and more new groups emerging.

Of the 100 questions on our leader survey one question (#94) showed the most significant correlation to small group growth. The question was: "A coach or pastor meets with me to personally encourage me as a leader." Small group leaders could respond to this using a five-point scale, indicating rarely, seldom, sometimes, often, or *very often*. If the leaders answered *often* or *very often* their small groups tended to be much healthier and faster growing.

Creating a strong coaching system takes time. For many churches it means creating a new culture of relational mentoring in their church. This is doable, but it takes persistence to get it working well. It involves recruiting and training your coaches and then overseeing them in a way that consistently supports, encourages and actively coaches them.

Jim Egli, Leadership Pastor of the Vineyard Church, Urbana, IL, author of Small Groups, Big Impact.

Myth:

Finding the Right Coaching Model Is the Key to Success

Somewhere along the way, coaching became another way to describe entire cell models. I've noticed when some people refer to a particular model they are actually talking about a coaching structure. Some might say, "I follow the Cho model." What they're actually saying is that they have organized their cell coaching or supervisory system according to geography, like David Cho.

When people say, "I follow the G12 model," they usually mean that they have decided to organize their coaching in groups of twelve using homogeneous networks. Each cell leader would be in a coaching group of one to twelve other cell leaders in specific categories, such as men, women, or youth.

Because people have connected church growth with these coaching structures, it's easy to assume that the coaching structure itself will make the church growth happen. Can a coaching structure bring growth?

Truth:

The Relationship between the Coach and the Coachee Is More Important Than the Structure

What makes coaching effective has little to do with the actual coaching structure and everything to do with the relationship between coach and coachee. I refer to this relationship as the "content of coaching."

I've written various books on coaching structures, but the most important coaching book I've written is entitled *How to Be a Great Cell Group Coach*.[15] In that book I talk about how a coach needs to be a good prayer warrior, listener, encourager, developer, strategist, and confronter. These are the characteristics that make or break coaching, not its structure.

A coaching structure might dictate that Harry and Joe meet at a certain time every week or that Harry supervises five cell leaders. The coaching content, however, is that Harry cares for and ministers to Joe.

Coaching structure should be as simple as possible. If a church planter begins a cell church, the church planter will coach all the new leaders. When there are ten cell leaders, it's time to train two supervisors to help with the coaching load. As the cells increase and the church grows, the supervisory structure will also expand.

Myth:

Coaches Only Listen and Ask Questions

Most of the coaching literature highlights the coach's role as reflecting information back to the coachee. The coach is called to listen, ask questions, and guide the coachee to make his or her own decisions. This is good and right. The coach should place the coachee in the driver's seat. The coach is not the authority or the consultant. While listening and asking questions are essential for effective coaching, is it possible to limit coaching by only focusing on these truths?

Truth:

The Coach Seeks to Equip the Group Leader with Whatever It Takes

In the last ten years, the most important principle I've learned about coaching is what I call, "throwing out the rulebook," or put more positively, "using everything in the toolbox."

I've discovered that sometimes I have to confront and challenge a coachee. Other times, I listen to the coachee's concerns about cell church, ministry in general, or personal struggles. I have found there are times when I need to tell the coachee to go back and re-read a book that has the answers to his or her concerns. I've learned to create different approaches as new circumstances arise.

I have found I have to bring my entire self to the table when coaching. I'm not just focusing on one aspect of my life but the entire spectrum (e.g., personality, upbringing, cell experience, and knowledge). Whatever I can draw from, I use. I'm not just pulling out my PowerPoints, my cell notes, or coaching rules; I'm giving my whole self.

My goal is to serve the leader, and so I ruthlessly place his or her agenda as the top priority. I'm sure this is also true in coaching a sport like tennis. ESPN wrote about coaching tennis stars, like Federer, saying:

> In today's game, most players—top stars as well as journeymen—put great stock in having a full-time dedicated coach as an appendage. The role of a coach can vary from tactician and strategy expert to psychologist, travel agent, babysitter, substitute parent, and best friend, and often is comprised of all those facets.[16]

The phrase *all of those facets* is critical. There's no one way to do coaching. The best coaching is comprised of *all of those facets*. For example, I spend a lot of time praying, listening, and waiting on God before I coach. I bring my spiritual life into the relationship.

I also bring my own character and my relational skills. How I relate to people will come out in my coaching. I also do my best to be the coachee's friend.

Sometimes, the most important thing I can do is engage in lighthearted conversation, laughter, or just have fun together.

While coaching, I relate what has worked for me and what has not worked for me, but I also share knowledge of what others have done, books written that apply to the problem, and online information that often provides more help than what I've tested or personally experienced. Often an illustration will jump out at me, and I share it with the one I'm coaching.

I think the coach short-changes the coachee by limiting the coaching roles. Some coachees simply need knowledge. They need to be taught how to lead a cell group. At other times, the coachee needs to share about struggles at work or with family.

God-inspired coaching is all about servanthood. It's all about serving the coachee and making him or her successful. The coach does what it takes to bless the coachee. Is it a listening ear? The coach is ready. Is it consulting? The coach will give it. Is it teaching? The coach is willing.

Eleven
TRANSITION MYTHS AND TRUTHS

Dear Mr. Boren,

It seems to me that the way a church transitions from a traditional church to a cell church is a crucial strategic move. However, it seems that many churches just jump into the cell group strategy without really thinking that much about the transition process. Could you help me understand what's going on in a church transition?

Sincerely,

Pastor Ron

Dear Pastor Ron,

I wish I could give a computer chip to pastors that would automatically make them rethink their assumptions and expectations about how to transition their churches. So many these days are taking the franchise approach to cell group implementation. They buy into the pre-packaged model and then implement that model according to the instructions of the franchiser. But when you do this, it assumes that the change is tactical in nature. In other words, it assumes that the church can change, if you simply readjust the structures and operating procedures.

This approach, however, rarely leads us to the results we want. It fails to deal with "adaptive" or "deep" change. This kind of change deals with life habits, church values and cultural assumptions that are woven into the fabric of how a group of people operate—the things people do even when they are not aware of it.

When leaders fail to understand the difference between tactical (outward) change and adaptive (inward) change, they might change the structure but fail to lead people into a different way of being God's people. So many churches have started cell groups, but in reality, all they did was shift their Sunday school classes into homes and called them cells. They might have the right cell group structure, but they failed to see the need for cell church life.

Here are few key principles that might help guide you as you lead others into the cell church vision:

1. *Slow down.* It's always easier to speed up than put on the breaks.
2. *Start small.* Find a few innovative people who want to experiment with cell group life and help them do it. Mentor them. Learn how to do cell group life with them. Then allow that life to infect others as you start new groups.
3. *Don't force people to "get it."* Not everyone will embrace cell groups at the same rate. Some people will pick up on it quickly. Others will sit back and observe. Others will resist. This is normal. Avoid judging people. Just focus your energy on those who are ready for group life and let others see the reality of this new life. If you are patient, they will come around.
4. *Stay put.* It will take a few years to get this engrained into the fabric of church life. If you don't plan on staying at your church for more than four years, then you need to really think about whether transitioning the church to cells is a wise choice.
5. *Pray.* Build cell groups upon the foundation of prayer. The practice of intense prayer is common to every successful cell church. You can do a lot of things wrong in your transition. But don't let this be one of them.

I hope that these principles help you as you move forward. Many blessings on the journey.

Scott Boren,
author of various books and Director of the Center for Community and Mission, www.mscottboren.com

Myth:

Get Rid of the Programs Right Away

I receive many questions in my seminars about the place of programs or ministries in the cell church. Most churches that want to transition are overloaded with programs and want to know what to do with them. Some pastors become so excited about cell church that they immediately want to get rid of all their programs and ministries. Others aren't so sure because they know those programs are meeting important needs in the church. What should they do?

Truth:

Wait until You Have Enough Cells to Cut Out Programs

I counsel pastors not to uproot any programs during the initial stages of the cell transition. After all, the existing programs serve important needs. People find fellowship in those programs as well as the ability to exercise their spiritual muscles. When cells begin to take root, however, there won't be the same need for those programs.

The church won't need an evangelism program, for example, when the cells start evangelizing. Yet only when the cells are present and evangelizing should the church delete the evangelism program. The same is true with discipleship. Many programs support discipleship in the church. However, when cells are caring for the leaders and discipling the members through the equipping track, there is no longer the same need for a discipleship program.

I do counsel pastors not to add new programs once they start on the cell journey. Cell members need time to focus on going through the training, getting to know non-Christians, and ministering to those in the cell group. If the church starts adding additional programs and ministries, the cell emphasis will be diluted and people won't have the time to give cell ministry the necessary attention.

Myth:

Jump into Cell Church Immediately

The cell church strategy has so many benefits. Through the cells, a church can pastor the entire congregation. Cell church also makes sense from a biblical perspective because it helps members grow in relationships and accountability. Then there's the doctrinal factor. Most cell churches connect the pastor's teaching with the cell lesson. Most pastors are thrilled to have the congregation apply the Sunday sermon.

Because there are so many benefits, it's common for a pastor to come back from a cell seminar and make an immediate announcement about becoming a cell church. Is this wise?

Truth:

It's Best to Have a Long Term Transition Plan

I counsel pastors not to make a church-wide announcement until the church is in the process of transitioning. In reality, what would the pastor announce? A structural shift? People who haven't experienced cell life will interpret the announcement about becoming a cell church as just another program. This is counter-productive and will cause weariness in the congregation to have to work through another change in programs.

It's much better if the lead pastor and key leaders work out a long-term strategy behind the scenes that include time-tables, development of the equipping track, strategy for coaching, and how the leadership team will guide the cell vision. Such strategizing is part of the pre-transition stage of effective cell church transitions.

The actual transition starts when the lead pastor facilitates a pilot group. This pilot group normally meets for six months to a year. Those in the group are strong believers who are willing to lead their own cell group when the pilot group gives birth. In the pilot group, the lead pastor demonstrates how to lead a cell by doing it. Before the pilot group multiplies, the lead pastor will attempt evangelistic outreach with the new believers going to the new cell groups.

After the pilot group multiplies, the lead pastor can make an announcement about the new cell groups in the church.

Carefully laid out plans are always better than ones that are made in a hurry. Remember the tortoise and the hare. The hare ran out quickly, confidently, and arrogantly. The tortoise's strategy paid off in the long run, and he crossed the finish line first.

One large traditional church in New York became excited about cell church ministry. As I helped them plan their transition, the senior pastor instinctively articulated his own need to lead a pilot group to the staff and key leaders, so that he could model cell ministry and make sure his key leaders also understood it. He gathered staff members in his house while he led the first cell. This pastor understood the need to start right and that it was best for him to fix the problems in his pilot cell before those problems became part of the entire cell structure.

Just the opposite happened in another church I consulted. As I made initial contact with the lead pastor, it became clear that he didn't want to change anything in his program-based church. He liked the idea of the cell church strategy as an addition to what he was already doing, as long as he didn't have to be involved. He was only interested in the outward achievements that cell ministry might bring without paying any cost to make them a reality.

Myth:

You Must Start the Transition with One Prototype

I recommend starting the cell church transition with one pilot group, led by the senior pastor. Many of those churches that have successfully transitioned to the cell model have used this strategy with great effectiveness. Yet, is this the only way to transition to the cell church model?

Truth:

There are Various Ways to Transition

I remember a good friend, a pastor, who was turned off to cell ministry because certain cell gurus made it seem that you had to follow a long, complicated, and rules-bound system when starting the first pilot group. My friend was even told to close the existing groups and enter into a slow process of prototyping. He decided to quit because cell church seemed too complicated for him.

The Elim Church didn't start their transition with just one pilot group. Elim transitioned their entire church at the same time, which at that time numbered around three thousand people. Sergio Solorzano, the founding pastor and undisputed leader, instructed the small church plants to come together and begin a city-wide cell church. The small church pastors in San Salvador became the network of pastors that formed the one huge cell church in San Salvador.

Solorzano and his team gathered all leaders together on a regular basis to teach them cell principles, how to make the transition, and what they were supposed to do in the cell. Even with this teaching, the church had to "fail forward" and fine-tune their system many times as they moved forward. Although I would not suggest this strategy, it worked for Elim.

Phil Potter, rector of an Anglican church in the UK wrote a book entitled *The Challenge of the Cell Church*. In that book, he describes how his church made the transition to a cell church by starting ten cells simultaneously. How did he do it? He and the key leaders spent months talking about the transition to a cell church and then included the entire congregation in the process. When they were in total agreement, the church started ten cells at the same time. Potter's church was another exception to the normal rule of the senior pastor leading the first pilot group.

When we transitioned our church in Ecuador, we were only three and a half years old. The leaders who had established the church were still in place. Therefore, we could make changes more quickly. We started with several cells at once, although we did prioritize prototyping principles. Each of the pastors led cell groups and modeled to the rest of the church how to make cell groups work.[17]

Part of the reason we saw such rapid growth was because we counted the cost and were committed to the cell vision for the long-term.

I know another church in Ecuador that started with three pilot groups. The church knew a lot about small group ministry, and the pastoral staff was completely committed to the transition. They were a very large church and the lead pastor felt the liberty to start several pilot groups at once. It worked well for them. He led one and key staff members led the additional cell groups.

According to Scott Boren, who has done extensive research on transitioning to the cell church strategy, every church that has successfully transitioned and is moving forward in cell ministry has followed prototyping principles, even though they may not have prototyped with just one cell group. Boren noticed that effective cell churches don't wait for perfection before they start moving ahead with starting new cells. They understood the need to learn as they go.

People will do what they see, so a church must have prototype principles in mind when making the transition. There are, however, various ways to do this.

Twelve
CHURCH PLANTING MYTHS AND TRUTHS

Dear Pastor Seibert,

I've admired from a distance how your church has launched new cell churches around the world. I'm trying to discern God's call on my life about whether to plant a new cell church in my city. I was wondering how you see the cell working with the weekend celebration in new church plants. I'd love to hear how this works itself out in new church plants that are a part of the Antioch network.

Thanks for your time,

Pastor Josh

Dear Pastor Josh,

First of all let me say that the centrality of the church is the person of Jesus Christ. Without the love and the power of Jesus pulsating through your personal life, we don't have the strength or the confidence to plant what God would have for us. So my first challenge to all our church planters is to make sure that their time with Jesus in the word, worship, and prayer is the number one priority every day. We train church planters to organize their days around this place of meeting with God, to pour out their hearts, to hear from God, and to respond to God consistently. A leader's devotional life must be shaped by not only waiting on God and asking him for wisdom for the day, but also asking for specific direction. When you are creating something out of nothing, as in starting a new church, it is so important that the creator is in charge of that journey.

One little practical exercise that I have used through the years to help me wait on God is basically "God, could you give me three things to do today?" We can't accomplish everything every day, but we can accomplish three things. God has been faithful to show me what he wants me to do, and as I have followed through, the results have been encouraging.

From a strategic perspective, remember we are trying to build a discipleship movement. Matthew 28:19-20 says, "Go therefore and make disciples of all the nations, baptizing them in the name of the Father and the Son and the Holy Spirit, teaching them to observe all that I commanded you; and lo, I am with you always, even to the end of the age." Discipleship movements begin by investing in the lives of people in such a way that they are investing in others. What I mean by this is to sow the seeds of the gospel into others, so that they in turn will do the same. That is why the Sunday celebration is not the central piece of the new church plant. When the celebration becomes the center piece of the new church plant, everything revolves around the crowd, which makes it very difficult to become a discipleship movement. But if relationship and discipleship is the beginning of the church plant, then you come to celebrate what God has already been doing throughout the week in each other's lives.

It takes longer and more of your time and energy to invest in people's lives, than to invest everything into the celebration, but you'll never regret building a great foundation for all that God wants to do. When we first started Antioch in 1999, we were meeting in rented facilities and because of that we solely relied on our life groups. The life groups communicated with our people about where the celebration gatherings would be held.

We often had more people in our life groups then we did on Sunday mornings because the life groups were taking responsibility for people's lives. I was challenged early on by people asking for different types of programs. We purposely decided that for two years we would simply offer life groups and a Sunday celebration. All the things that people had in their hearts: to reach out to the poor, to care for widows, to provide financially for someone in need, we purposely implemented in the context of the life groups. We wanted our life groups to become little house churches so that everyone would be pastored and feel responsible to minister.

The best advice I can give you is that it begins and ends with the church planter. We often tell our guys, when they are starting a church plant, to do a 100-day push. It's common knowledge that a president will chart his course in the first 100 days of the presidency. We have seen the same thing in church planting.

Once you and your family are settled, those first three months should be spent sharing the gospel every day, sharing your vision for what God is doing everyday, and beginning to invest immediately in hungry, teachable people. Invite these people into a small group community and empower them to reach others as well.

May God bless you as you take your next steps toward cell church life.

Jimmy Seibert,
Lead Pastor of Antioch Community Church, www.antiochcc.net

Myth:

The Focus Should Be on the Success of a Singular Church

I'll never forget the experience of sitting in the audience at Fuller Seminary in 1984 and hearing David Cho talk about his four hundred thousand member church. I was a struggling pioneer church planter in downtown Long Beach, and his words seemed surreal as he talked about the effectiveness of his cell system to both pastor the people and evangelize new ones. I wanted to be just like David Cho. I bought his tapes, new book, and taught my people about home cell groups.

Later I had the opportunity to visit Cho's church and many huge cell churches like Yoido Full Gospel Church. All the huge churches I visited were keenly impacted by the incredible growth in Korea. Yet, are large mega-cell churches the exception or the rule?

Truth:

Planting New Smaller Cell Churches Is Desirable

Paul was the most effective church planter of the first century. He planted simple, reproducible churches and moved on to spread the gospel. He didn't stay in one place to grow one church larger and larger. Yet, he could say "So from Jerusalem all the way around to Illyricum, I have fully proclaimed the gospel of Christ" (Romans 15:19). Before AD 47 there were no churches in these provinces. In AD 57 Paul spoke of his work being accomplished.

Bob Roberts, Jr., senior pastor of Northwood Church in Texas, has planted one hundred some churches. In his book, *The Multiplying Church*, he writes:

> On more than one occasion, I've found myself in a group of mega-church pastors who make a statement like this: "We need to partner to start some significant churches—we don't need to waste our time on these little churches of a hundred or two hundred." They don't get it! I try to educate them, but, more often than not, to no avail. When they make a statement like that, they miss two things. First, they don't

know their history. Where faith has exploded, it has never been because of the multiplication of mega-churches, but of smaller churches from 50 to 200. . . Second, they don't understand the nature of movements. Movements are personal and viral. Where movements have emerged, it hasn't been because of the large, but because of the small.[18]

I am more and more convinced that we in the cell church world have done a great job of training leaders through cell ministry, but have not focused sufficiently on raising up pastors to multiply new churches. Christian Schwarz and his research team studied churches around the world and discovered that church plants were more effective than larger churches in leading people to become Christ-followers, baptizing members, and ministering to needs. Schwarz writes:

> If instead of a single church with 2,856 in worship we had 56 churches, each with 51 worshippers, these churches would, statistically win 1,792 new people within five years—16 times the number the mega-church would win. Thus we can conclude that the evangelistic effectiveness of mini-churches is statistically 1,600 percent greater than that of mega-churches! [19]

When Jesus saw the incredible needs around him and especially those who were helpless and harassed and in need of a shepherd, he said to his disciples, "The harvest is plentiful but the workers are few. Ask the Lord of the harvest, therefore, to send out workers into his harvest field" (Matthew 9:37-38).

The best church planters are those who have multiplied cell groups and supervised the new leaders. They possess the vital, needed experience to plant a church.

As I travel around the world, I passionately plead with larger cell churches to hear God's call for missions. I would love to see leaders who have multiplied cells and now supervise cells to consider becoming missionary church planters all over the world. Senior pastors are the key to releasing such people. Some of these multiplication pastors will plant nearby in the same city, state, or country. Others will become cross-cultural missionaries to plant cell churches on distant shores.

Myth:

The Church Starts When the Celebration Service Starts

Many people equate starting a church with the first large gathering that comes together to worship and hear the preaching of God's word. Many call this the first celebration service, which normally takes place on Sunday morning.

Some church planters might have small groups or teams in the beginning to prepare for the first large gathering, but these groups are a means to the end. The end goal is the large group gathering.

Truth:

The Church Starts When the First Cell Begins

In the cell church strategy, the first cell group is officially the church. The goal is to multiply cells and bring them together to celebrate.

One church planter started a home group and multiplied it several times. Yet, as I talked with him, he felt discouraged, saying, "I'm just not sure if I'm the one who should lead this church plant." I just listened. He continued, "I should have more people by now so that I can launch this church."

"But you already have a church," I countered.

"But I need to have a lot more people on the launch team to truly launch the church in the future," he replied.

Deeply ingrained in this church planter was the notion that his church really didn't exist until they had a major launch with many people. In the meantime, he was simply gathering people who were preparing to launch the real church. While he waited for the launch, he was weighted down by feelings of failure because others had told him that he should have more people in order to launch the church.

I counseled my friend to see his first cell as the church. I told him to enjoy the multiplication of individual cells, knowing that he had already planted the church. Eventually, he would bring those cells together in a celebration service to mature all the believers through worship and teaching God's word.

I wanted the church planter to feel the pure joy of knowing that he had already planted the church. Obviously his job was to steadily reach out, multiply cells, and continue to make disciples.

As written throughout the pages of this book, one of the foundational truths of the cell church is that the cell is the church. When the pastor launches the first cell, the church is established. The goal is to multiply the first cell into more cell groups and then to eventually gather those cells together to celebrate.

I mentored one doctoral student who wrote his dissertation about planting a simple church among the Christian Reformed denomination. He was looking for support and approval. He planned to begin with a one small group (cell) and multiply into more groups. His title, *A Strategy for Beginning a Church Multiplication Movement in Muskegon, Michigan*, declared his bold intentions.

But he first had to get his initial cell accepted as a real church. His denomination only considered a real church as one which had a pulpit, building, etc. My job as his mentor was to help him present the case that the cell is the church.[20]

The challenge for the doctoral student was to overcome the denominational rules that stated, "A minister of the Word serving as pastor of a congregation shall preach the Word, administer the sacraments, conduct public worship services, catechize the youth, and train members for Christian service."[21] Notice the words "conduct public worship services." Could he have a church without a public service? He planned to start the church with one small group. Was this one group not the church from the beginning? His struggle was not merely a theoretical exercise. He was looking for denominational funding and support.

He did successfully complete the dissertation and started the church as a single cell. It eventually grew into multiple cells and a celebration service.

I recommend starting the first cell on Saturday night or another evening during the week—not on Sunday morning. By doing this, it takes away some of the pressure to compete with larger Sunday morning churches in the area. I also counsel church planters to do training on Sunday morning, hold a prayer meeting, or do outreach. It's a great idea to mobilize the church to reach out and minister to those with need.

Myth:

Open the Celebration Service as Soon as Possible

I have heard that churches in Japan learned from North America that a true church has to have a celebration service. The first thing a church planter in Japan thinks about is opening up a celebration service. One Japanese church, for example, holds their celebration service with seven people present, complete with a pulpit and professional bulletins. The seven are sitting in rows. The ecclesiology behind this type of church planting is that the church is a place where people congregate to hear a preacher. A minister goes through intense training to become a pastor and then needs a place to use his training, namely in a building where people can sit and listen to him or her.

Even though a pastor might believe that the cell is the church, it's easy to feel pressured to open the celebration service as soon as possible.

One pastor in North Carolina felt that pressure and started a celebration service with only two families. He depended on these two families to do everything. The two families, along with the pastor and his wife, had to set up, take down, care for the children, lead worship, and provide refreshments. And it was always awkward to feel a sense of celebration when only a handful was present. This small team longed for more people but unfortunately, a crowd never formed, and they closed the church. But should they have gone through such pain in the first place?

Truth:

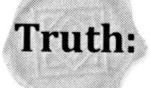

Wait until There Are Enough People in Cells to Start Weekly Celebration Services

Consider it a luxury if you can start a church with a large core from the mother church. We did this in Ecuador when one hundred fifty people and ten cell groups left the mother church to start a daughter church.

We also had a piece of land and building! We started running and the church never stopped. While this is an ideal scenario, it is difficult to reproduce and most churches don't start this way. Most cell church plants, in fact, start with a single cell and grow from there.

The celebration, when it takes place, is simply the congregating of the cells together. It's a time for the cells to celebrate. Most cell churches celebrate weekly, but I counsel churches to wait until they have enough cells and enough people in cells to do this. Otherwise, too much of the burden is placed upon a few key families to pay the bills, keep ministries going, and even provide key leadership positions.

I recommend starting weekly celebration when there are eight to ten cells and approximately seventy to one hundred people in those cells. Until that time, it's best to only celebrate periodically, say, once per month. Prayer meetings and social gatherings can be used to bring the cells together in the meantime. You might want to follow the schedule:

- 3 cells: once per month celebration
- 6 cells: twice per month celebration
- 8-10 cells: weekly celebration

In a home, it's comfortable to have a small gathering. A living room, holds about a dozen people. If only four show up, no one seems to mind. In fact, often a smaller group can share more intimately. This is not true in a celebration service. When only a few people show up, it's harder to create the atmosphere of celebration.

Myth:

You Must Start a Weekly Celebration Service

Some people believe that cell church must always have a weekly cell and a weekly celebration service. After all, isn't that what it means to be a two-winged church? I thought this way for many years and even taught that the definition of a cell church included weekly cells and weekly celebration. But should this always be true?

Truth:

Some Cell Churches Will Never Meet Weekly in Celebration

North American churches average about seventy-five people in weekly celebration services (I'm not sure about the weekly average of worldwide cell churches). Many cell churches will never grow beyond one hundred people. In *Where Do We Go From Here?*, Ralph Neighbour writes:

The recommendation is that you delay any celebration for the cells until you have a least one hundred to participate. The assignments to develop the services can then be rotated among the cells, or certain cells can be asked to perform the same tasks in each service. When you do finally create a public service, you'll focus them to build the life of the cells, rather than to attract people who may not be interested in cell life. The more converts you gather in, the faster you will see your vision become reality.[22]

I agree with Ralph Neighbour's counsel and believe that many cell churches will never have a weekly celebration meeting. Yes, the cells will meet each week, but the celebration service would only be held once per quarter, each month, or twice per month.

Bill Beckham, an expert in cell ministry, also believes that we need to be creative about the frequency and the purpose of the celebration service. For example, some cell churches will bring the cells together for a prayer meeting, training, and then for a monthly celebration service (e.g., worship, preaching, etc.).

By requiring a weekly celebration, we are limiting the number of church plants and church planters. Weekly celebration services, complete with preaching, worship, and children's ministry require certain skills that not all church planters possess. Some pastors simply don't have the charisma or talent to do so. I am convinced that we're not church planting more often because some people insist that church planters need to preach at a weekly celebration service.[23]

Run with Truth

Some of the myths in this book are the result of good intentions gone astray. A church or pastor might have tried to correct an imbalance but instead became part of the problem. Yet, other myths are inspired by the enemy with the goal of thwarting and destroying the work of God.

On June 09, 1999 I received a prophesy from Harold Weitz, an anointed South African cell church pastor who has a proven gift of prophesy. Part of the prophesy said:

"The enemy is woeful of this one thing: to stop the move of all the cell churches; for the Lord says, I will take my church back to the Bible pattern of the church of house to house."

When God moves and creates a strategy that brings health and life to his church, Satan and his demons often bring deception to thwart God's work. Jesus, in fact, tells us to watch out for the false prophets who come in sheep's clothing, but have the inward intention of wolves. Jesus told us that we would recognize them by their fruit (Matthew 7:15-16).

My hope is that as a result of reading this book, you will be better equipped to discern the enemy's errors from God's principles, the tares from the wheat.

More importantly, I desire that you will confidently run with positive principles and insight that will allow you to build a strong foundation for your cell ministry. I pray that you will take the biblical, time-tested principles expounded in this book and discover the path that leads to long-term, fruitful cell ministry.

AFTERWORD
BY CARL GEORGE

Joel Comiskey is someone I have admired for many years. His invitation to add an afterthought to this excellent book is a privilege I cherish.

The direction of cell groups for the future has become clearer with each passing decade. Churches cannot build enough facilities to keep up with their worship needs, much less classrooms for Christian education.

Christianity has spread rapidly under persecution and without government sponsorship from the days of the early church until now. The largest churches in existence, now found on virtually every continent, are relying on variations of cell group models to care for and nurture their converts. The jury is no longer out. The verdict is clear. Cell group ministry works.

The only impediments to implementing cell group ministry are lack of clarity about goals and distractions from other pursuits. I have watched cell group efforts fail only because of insufficient leadership wisdom and perseverance to work through the resistances and impediments encountered in the transition. With this book, clarity is assured.

Joel and I both met David Cho in 1984. We both have drawn much inspiration from his pioneering work in Korea.

When Cho explained the roots of his cell church strategy, he gave credit to several streams that led to the foundation for the largest church in the history of Christendom:

1. His mother-in-law's pioneering influence when he was too ill to conduct business as usual.
2. His exposure to the history of John Wesley, whose class meetings (actually home groups) maintained the fruit that established churches could not.
3. His early successes with using staff member to coach and support the cell leaders.

All three of these core principles helped Cho develop his small group ministry as his church grew larger and larger.

When Cho expounded on the place of faith and prayer in obeying God's call to open up cell groups, he said something that has rung in my ears for many years. In fact, I can still hear Cho saying, "It is the cell *system* that you must understand."

By these words, Cho conveyed to me something that goes beyond the cell itself. It's the idea that cells are not an end in themselves. If you only focused on cells, you would miss important truths that Cho fully grasped:

1. New believers receive personal attention in cells. Cho realized that new Christians matured into disciples of Jesus with the attention provided through cell ministry.

2. New leaders are developed through cell ministry. Cho realized that cells developed leaders who in turn started new cells. He then employed staff pastors to come alongside the cell leaders.

The kind of leader Cho had in mind is described by Joel as a *disciple-maker*. This kind of host, facilitator, gatherer, leader, or whatever you eventually call him or her, has a bigger vision than the cell meeting. *Disciple-makers* envision fully mature cell members who are developing new disciples through cell ministry.

Dr. Comiskey has engaged us in a conversation about cell church that takes us far down the road toward effectiveness. By using the format of debunking myths and by presenting questions from real life ministers, Joel opens to us a path for managing the crucial challenges facing implementation of cell ministry. His writings help us to skirt obstacles imposed by rigid adherence to formulas and traditions. He holds out hope, not just to the megachurch leader, but to the church planter and the smaller congregation pastor as well. His presentation is so inspiring that I find myself mentally nominating my own neighbors and recent acquaintances for invitations to a cell meeting in my own home!

Myths and Truths follows his excellent book, *Leadership Explosion*. I cannot think of a more helpful pair of books than these two for anyone hoping to maximize fruitfulness in cell ministry within their congregation.

Carl George
Consulting for Growth
Taylors (Greenville) SC

APPENDIX

In May 2005, Joel Comiskey Group commissioned the Natural Church Development research center in Germany to do a statistical study that compared North American cell churches with North American non-cell churches. At the time, NCD had 7,972 church profiles from North America. Out of that number 3.6% qualified as cell-churches. Although the percentage of cell churches is comparatively small, statistical data software enables researchers to level the playing field in order to make exact comparisons.

In this appendix, I'll simply quote the research of Christoph Schalk from the analysis he sent. To receive a complete analysis in PDF format, email info@joelcomiskeygroup.com.

Definition of cell church according to NCD

NCD defines a cell church as a church with more than 75% of members involved in holistic small groups.

Schalk told me, Joel Comiskey, that their research team classified a cell church as a church with a score of 65 or higher in holistic small groups *and* with more than 75% of worship attendance in small groups. For the sake of emphasis, let me say this another way: in churches labeled cell churches by this study, more than 75% of those who attended weekend worship also attended holistic small groups during the week, and these churches excelled in holistic small groups by scoring higher than 65 in the NCD testing.[24]

This still doesn't define, however, what a holistic small group is according to NCD. The answer to this question can be found in the book *Natural Church Development*, where the characteristics of a holistic small group include the following:

- Emphasis on the application of biblical truth that leads to transformation. People in these small groups have the liberty to bring up issues that apply to daily life.
- Exercise of spiritual gifts within the small group.
- Priority of small groups as being just as important as the celebration service. The small group, in other words, is not simply a programmatic extension of the celebration service. Schwarz uses the term "mini-church" to describe a holistic small group.
- Multiplication: multiplication stood out as the key factor in healthy, growing churches. Schwarz says, "If we were to identify any one principle as the most important . . . then without a doubt it would be the multiplication of small groups." Schwarz continues, "Continuous

multiplication of small groups is a universal church growth principle."[25]

The NCD definition of a holistic small group is very close to the cell definition given in the introduction of this book. I also like their definition of a cell church and believe it's an excellent starting point. I have appreciated the ministry of NCD, and I'm encouraged to see that their extensive research is confirming that cell church ministry is a healthy strategy for church growth.[26]

NA cell churches scored higher in all categories

According to their research analysis of North American cell churches and non-cell churches, Schalk says, "Cell churches overall scored significantly higher in all areas surveyed than non-cell churches. Combined cell church scores averaged 58 while combined non-cell church scores averaged 50."

The "Inspiring Worship" category showed the smallest difference (2 points higher for cell churches) and "Holistic Small Groups" showed the most difference (17 points higher for cell churches).

Better large group worship

Yet Schalk points out that even churches who say they would focus on small groups over large group worship still had better scores for large group worship. He says, "This finding indicates that cells don't detract from corporate worship—they add to it. Additionally, the rate of church planting—in spite of the fact that the cell church movement has seemed to focus on getting larger rather than on planting more churches—would seem to indicate that multiplication is in fact in the genetic code."

Higher growth rate

The study showed that cell churches demonstrated an average growth rate more than double that of non-cell churches.

Conclusion

Taking the time to build a God-honoring church that is making disciples is not easy. But Jesus did tell us to count the cost. The NCD study challenges us to grow a church from the inside out—one that produces lasting, fruitful growth. Growing healthy churches through the cell church strategy is vital to get the North American church back on track. Thankfully, many churches in North America are already successfully implementing the cell church strategy (http://www.joelcomiskeygroup.com/articles/worldwide/NorthAmerica.htm). They can inspire and give insight to those who want to follow in their steps.

ENDNOTES

1. Accessed on Tuesday, March 29, 2011 at http://hirr.hartsem.edu/research/fastfacts/fast_facts.html#sizecong
2. Joel Comiskey, Sam Scaggs, Ben Wong, *You Can Coach* (Moreno Valley: CA: CCS Publishing, 2010), pp. 70-71.
3. For more on this topic, read pp. 46–48 of *Natural Church Development* (Carol Stream, IL: ChurchSmart Resources, 1996).
4. John Kotter, *A Sense of Urgency* (Harvard, MI: Harvard Business Press, 2008), introduction. Kindle Edition.
5. Elim knows each week how many cells met, how many attended cells, number of conversions in cells, baptisms, and how many people the cell leaders visited. When the results are below expectations, Elim prays hader, makes mid-course corrections, and seeks to mobilize the troops for battle.
6. *The Spirit-Filled Small Group* and *Discover* both discuss how the gifts of the Spirit are best discovered in the small group atmosphere. All of the passages in scripture about the gifts of the Spirit were written to house

churches. These books can be purchased at www.joelcomiskeygroup.com.

7. The injunction not to take bribes is several times repeated in the Bible, twice with the reason given that "bribes blind the clear-sighted and upset the pleas of the just" (Ex. 23:8; Deut. 16:19). The warning is also sounded that the taking of bribes might lead to the shedding of innocent blood (Deut. 27:25). God is praised as being unreceptive to bribes (Deut. 10:17, et al.), and as human judges are generally exhorted to imitate divine qualities, so they are urged to be impartial, and not susceptible to bribes (II Chron. 19:7). The donor of bribes is blamed as a tempter or accomplice of the taker, transgressing the injunction "you shall not place a stumbling block before the blind" (Lev. 19:14). Bribery seems to have been rather widespread (cf. I Sam. 8:3), or else the prophets would hardly have denounced it so vehemently (Isa. 1:23; 5:23; 33:15; Ezek. 22:12; Amos 5:12; Micah 7:3), but it was in the nature of unethical misconduct rather than of a criminal offense [these verses are taken from http://www.jewishvirtuallibrary.org/jsource/judaica/ejud_0002_0004_0_03532.html]

8. Lawrence Khong, *The Apostolic Cell Church: Practical Strategies for Growth and Outreach from the Story of Faith Community Baptist Church* (Singapore: Touch Ministries International, 2000), p 32.

9. *Boundaries* (Grand Rapids, MI: Zondervan, 1992), pp. 99-100.

10. This compilation is credited to Jack Canfield and Mark Victor Hansen. They are the creators of the Chicken Soup empire and their book idea was rejected by almost every publisher. Posted by Carmen Leal on Thursday, July 29, 2004 on Writer's View, a yahoo group list.

11. John Mallison, *Growing Christians in Small Groups* (London: Scripture Union,1989), p. 5.

12. C. Kirk Hadaway, Francis M. DuBose, and Stuart A. Wright, *Home Cell Groups and House Churches* (Nashville, TN: Broadman Press, 1987), p. 40.

13. Jim Egli, Dwight Marble, *Small Groups, Big Impact: Connecting People to God and One Another in Thriving Groups* (Saint Charles, IL: ChurchSmart, 2011), p. 42.

14. Jeff Tunnell, blog on Joel Comiskey Group website on Monday, November 22, 2010, http://joelcomiskeygroup.com/blog_2/2010/11/22/multiplication-journey/

15. My books on coaching structure include: *Groups of Twelve, From Twelve to Three*, and *Passion and Persistence*. These books cover the three main coaching structures.

16. Accessed article at http://sports.espn.go.com/sports/tennis/wimbledon08/columns/story?columnist=harwitt_sandra&id=3473761

17. I remember the meeting in which as a pastoral staff we decided to oversee the twenty cells that we had at the time. Each staff committed himself to lead a cell, coach four existing cells, raise up coaches from within, report on how the cells were doing, and especially multiply the groups. As a pastoral team, we came together each week to chart the progress of the cells and to pastor the cell strategy together.

18.   Bob Roberts, Jr., *The Multiplying Church: The New Math for Starting New Churches* (Grand Rapids, MI: Zondervan, 2008), p. 65. 18.   For more on this topic, read pp. 46-48 of Natural Church Development (Carol Stream, IL: ChurchSmart Resources, 1996).

19. Ibid.

20. DeRidder and Hofman, *Manual of Christian Reformed Church Government*, p. 101.

21. Ralph Neighbour, *Where Do We Go From Here?* (Houston, TX: Touch Publications, 2000), p. 382.

22. As mentioned earlier, some pastors will prefer to gather the cells in a monthly celebration service, monthly half-night prayer meeting, and various social outreach or social outings.

23.   Personal correspondence with Christoph Schalk, Tuesday, August 31, 2004, who said there were 30,157,711 data entries in the NCD database.

24.   Christian Schwarz, Natural Church Development (Carol Steam, IL: ChurchSmart Resources, 1996), p. 32.

25. Brickman, *Natural Church Development and Cell Church: Friend or Foe?* On page 8 he says, "I am suggesting a marriage between the principles of cell church and Natural Church Development. I am suggesting not only compatibility, but I am suggesting that if a cell church paradigm can chase a thousand, the union of a cell church paradigm with the NCD paradigm can chase ten thousand. The whole will be far greater than the sum of the parts."

RESOURCES BY JOEL COMISKEY

Joel Comiskey's previous books cover the following topics

- Leading a cell group (How to Lead a Great Cell Group Meeting, 2001, 2009).
- How to multiply the cell group (Home Cell Group Explosion, 1998).
- How to prepare spiritually for cell ministry (An Appointment with the King, 2002, 2011).
- How to practically organize your cell system (Reap the Harvest,1999; Cell Church Explosion, 2004).
- How to train future cell leaders (Leadership Explosion, 2001; Live, 2007; Encounter, 2007; Grow, 2007; Share, 2007; Lead, 2007; Coach, 2008; Discover, 2008).
- How to coach/care for cell leaders (How to be a Great Cell Group Coach, 2003; Groups of Twelve, 2000; From Twelve to Three, 2002).
- How the gifts of the Spirit work within the cell group (The Spirit-filled Small Group, 2005, 2009; Discover, 2008).
- How to fine tune your cell system (Making Cell Groups Work Navigation Guide, 2003).
- Principles from the second largest church in the world (Passion and Persistence, 2004).
- How cell church works in North America (The Church that Multiplies, 2007, 2009).
- How to plant a church (Planting Churches that Reproduce, 2009)
- How to be a relational disciple (Relational Disciple, 2010).

All of the books listed are available from *Joel Comiskey Group* **by calling toll-free 1-888-344-CELL (2355) or by ordering at:**
www.joelcomiskeygroup.com

How To Lead A Great Cell Group Meeting: *So People Want to Come Back*

Do people expectantly return to your group meetings every week? Do you have fun and experience joy during your meetings? Is everyone participating in discussion and ministry? You can lead a great cell group meeting, one that is life changing and dynamic. Most people don't realize that they can create a God-filled atmosphere because they don't know how. Now the secret is out. This guide will show you how to:

- Prepare yourself spiritually to hear God during the meeting
- Structure the meeting so it flows
- Spur people in the group to participate and share their lives openly
- Share your life with others in the group
- Create stimulating questions
- Listen effectively to discover what is transpiring in others' lives
- Encourage and edify group members
- Open the group to non-Christians
- See the details that create a warm atmosphere

By implementing these time-tested ideas, your group meetings will become the hot-item of your members' week. They will go home wanting more and return each week bringing new people with them. 140 pgs.

Home Cell Group Explosion: *How Your Small Group Can Grow and Multiply*

The book crystallizes the author's findings in some eighteen areas of research, based on a meticulous questionnaire that he submitted to cell church leaders in eight countries around the world, locations that he also visited personally for his research. The detailed notes in the back of the book offer the student of cell church growth a rich mine for further reading. The beauty of Comiskey's book is that he not only summarizes his survey results in a thoroughly convincing way but goes on to analyze in practical ways many of his survey results in separate chapters. The happy result is that any cell church leader, intern or member completing this quick read will have his priorities/values clearly aligned and ready to be followed-up. If you are a pastor or small group leader, you should devour this book! It will encourage you and give you simple, practical steps for dynamic small group life and growth. 175 pgs.

Recources by Joel Comiskey

An Appointment with the King: *Ideas for Jump-Starting Your Devotional Life*

With full calendars and long lists of things to do, people often put on hold life's most important goal: building an intimate relationship with God. Often, believers wish to pursue the goal but are not sure how to do it. They feel frustrated or guilty when their attempts at personal devotions seem empty and unfruitful. With warm, encouraging writing, Joel Comiskey guides readers on how to set a daily appointment with the King and make it an exciting time they will look forward to. This book first answers the question "Where do I start?" with step-by-step instructions on how to spend time with God and practical ideas for experiencing him more fully. Second, it highlights the benefits of spending time with God, including joy, victory over sin, and spiritual guidance. The book will help Christians tap into God's resources on a daily basis, so that even in the midst of busyness they can walk with him in intimacy and abundance. 175 pgs.

Reap the Harvest: *How a Small Group System Can Grow Your Church*

Have you tried small groups and hit a brick wall? Have you wondered why your groups are not producing the fruit that was promised? Are you looking to make your small groups more effective? Cell-church specialist and pastor Dr. Joel Comiskey studied the world's most successful cell churches to determine why they grow. The key: They have embraced specific principles. Conversely, churches that do not embrace these same principles have problems with their groups and therefore do not grow. Cell churches are successful not because they have small groups but because they can support the groups. In this book, you will discover how these systems work. 236 pgs.

La Explosión de la Iglesia Celular: *Cómo Estructurar la Iglesia en Células Eficaces* (Editorial Clie, 2004)

This book is only available in Spanish and contains Joel Comiskey's research of eight of the world's largest cell churches, five of which reside in Latin America. It details how to make the transition from a traditional church to the cell church structure and many other valuable insights, including: the history of the cell church, how to organize your church to become a praying church, the most important principles of the cell church, and how to raise up an army of cell leaders. 236 pgs.

Leadership Explosion: *Multiplying Cell Group Leaders to Reap the Harvest*

Some have said that cell groups are leader breeders. Yet even the best cell groups often have a leadership shortage. This shortage impedes growth and much of the harvest goes untouched. Joel Comiskey has discovered why some churches are better at raising up new cell leaders than others. These churches do more than pray and hope for new leaders. They have an intentional strategy, a plan that will quickly equip as many new leaders as possible. In this book, you will discover the training models these churches use to multiply leaders. You will discover the underlying principles of these models so that you can apply them. 202 pgs.

FIVE-BOOK EQUIPPING SERIES

#1: Live   #2: Encounter   #3: Grow   #4: Share   #5: Lead

The five book equipping series is designed to train a new believer all the way to leading his or her own cell group. Each of the five books contains eight lessons. Each lesson has interactive activities that helps the trainee reflect on the lesson in a personal, practical way.

Live starts the training by covering key Christian doctrines, including baptism and the Lord's supper. 85 pgs.

Encounter guides the believer to receive freedom from sinful bondages. The Encounter book can be used one-on-one or in a group. 91 pgs.

Grow gives step-by-step instruction for having a daily quiet time, so that the believer will be able to feed him or herself through spending daily time with God. 87 pgs.

Share instructs the believer how to communicate the gospel message in a winsome, personal way. This book also has two chapters on small group evangelism. 91 pgs.

Lead prepares the Christian on how to facilitate an effective cell group. This book would be great for those who form part of a small group team. 91 pgs.

TWO-BOOK ADVANCED TRAINING SERIES

COACH   DISCOVER

Coach* and *Discover make-up the Advanced Training, prepared specifically to take a believer to the next level of maturity in Christ.

Coach prepares a believer to coach another cell leader. Those experienced in cell ministry often lack understanding on how to coach someone else. This book provides step-by-step instruction on how to coach a new cell leader from the first meeting all the way to giving birth to a new group. The book is divided into eight lessons, which are interactive and help the potential coach deal with real-life, practical coaching issues. 85 pgs.

Discover clarifies the twenty gifts of the Spirit mentioned in the New Testament. The second part shows the believer how to find and use his or her particular gift. This book is excellent to equip cell leaders to discover the giftedness of each member in the group. 91 pgs.

How to be a Great Cell Group Coach:
Practical insight for Supporting and Mentoring Cell Group Leaders

Research has proven that the greatest contributor to cell group success is the quality of coaching provided for cell group leaders. Many are serving in the position of a coach, but they don't fully understand what they are supposed to do in this position. Joel Comiskey has identified seven habits of great cell group coaches. These include: Receiving from God, Listening to the needs of the cell group leader, Encouraging the cell group leader, Caring for the multiple aspects of a leader's life, Developing the cell leader in various aspects of leadership, Strategizing with the cell leader to create a plan, Challenging the cell leader to grow.

Practical insights on how to develop these seven habits are outlined in section one. Section two addresses how to polish your skills as a coach with instructions on diagnosing problems in a cell group, how to lead coaching meetings, and what to do when visiting a cell group meeting. This book will prepare you to be a great cell group coach, one who mentors, supports, and guides cell group leaders into great ministry. 139 pgs.

Groups of Twelve: *A New Way to Mobilize Leaders and Multiply Groups in Your Church*

This book clears the confusion about the Groups of 12 model. Joel dug deeply into the International Charismatic Mission in Bogota, Colombia and other G12 churches to learn the simple principles that G12 has to offer your church. This book also contrasts the G12 model with the classic 5x5 and shows you what to do with this new model of ministry. Through onsite research, international case studies, and practical experience, Joel Comiskey outlines the G12 principles that your church can use today.

Billy Hornsby, director of the Association of Related Churches, says, "Joel Comiskey shares insights as a leader who has himself raised up numerous leaders. From how to recognize potential leaders to cell leader training to time-tested principles of leadership--this book has it all. The accurate comparisons of various training models make it a great resource for those who desire more leaders. Great book!" 182 pgs.

From Twelve To Three: *How to Apply G12 Principles in Your Church*

The concept of the Groups of 12 began in Bogota, Colombia, but now it is sweeping the globe. Joel Comiskey has spent years researching the G12 structure and the principles behind it.

From his experience as a pastor, trainer, and consultant, he has discovered that there are two ways to embrace the G12 concept: adopting the entire model or applying the principles that support the model.

This book focuses on the application of principles rather than adoption of the entire model. It outlines the principles and provides a modified application which Joel calls the G12.3. This approach presents a pattern that is adaptable to many different church contexts.

The concluding section illustrates how to implement the G12.3 in various kinds of churches, including church plants, small churches, large churches, and churches that already have cells. 178 pgs.

Recources by Joel Comiskey

The Spirit-filled Small Group: *Leading Your Group to Experience the Spiritual Gifts.* The focus in many of today's small groups has shifted from Spirit-led transformation to just another teacher-student Bible study. But exercising every member's spiritual gifts is vital to the effectiveness of the group. With insight born of experience in more than twenty years of small group ministry, Joel Comiskey explains how leaders and participants alike can be supernaturally equipped to deal with real-life issues. Put these principles into practice and your small group will never be the same!

This book works well with Comiskey's training book, **Discover.** It fleshes out many of the principles in Comiskey's training book. Chuck Crismier, radio host, Viewpoint, writes, "Joel Comiskey has again provided the Body of Christ with an important tool to see God's Kingdom revealed in and through small groups." 191 pgs.

Making Cell Groups Work Navigation Guide: *A Toolbox of Ideas and Strategies for Transforming Your Church.* For the first time, experts in cell group ministry have come together to provide you with a 600 page reference tool like no other. When Ralph Neighbour, Bill Beckham, Joel Comiskey and Randall Neighbour compiled new articles and information under careful orchestration and in-depth understanding that Scott Boren brings to the table, it's as powerful as private consulting! Joel Comiskey has an entire book within this mammoth 600 page work. There are also four additional authors.

Passion and Persistence: *How the Elim Church's Cell Groups Penetrated an Entire City for Jesus*

This book describes how the Elim Church in San Salvador grew from a small group to 116,000 people in 10,000 cell groups. Comiskey takes the principles from Elim and applies them to churches in North America and all over the world. Ralph Neighbour says: "I believe this book will be remember as one of the most important ever written about a cell church movement! I experienced the *passion* when visiting Elim many years ago. Comiskey's report about Elim is not a *pattern* to be slavishly copied. It is a journey into grasping the true theology and methodology of the New Testament church. You'll discover how the Elim Church fans into flame their passion for Jesus and His Word, how they organize their cells to penetrate a city and world for Jesus, and how they persist until God brings the fruit." 158 pgs.

The Church that Multiplies: *Growing a Healthy Cell Church in North America*

Does the cell church strategy work in North America? We hear about exciting cell churches in Colombia and Korea, but where are the dynamic North American cell churches? This book not only declares that the cell church concept does work in North America but dedicates an entire chapter to examining North American churches that are successfully using the cell strategy to grow in quality and quantity. This book provides the latest statistical research about the North American church and explains why the cell church approach restores health and growth to the church today. More than anything else, this book will provide practical solutions for pastors and lay leaders to use in implementing cell-based ministry. 181 pgs.

Planting Churches that Reproduce: *Planting a Network of Simple Churchces*

What is the best way to plant churches in the 21st century? Comiskey believes that simple, reproducible church planting is most effective. The key is to plant churches that are simple enough to grow into a movement of churches. Comiskey has been gathering material for this book for the past fifteen Years. He has also planted three churches in a wide variety of settings. Planting Churches that Reproduce is the fruit of his research and personal experience. Comiskey uses the latest North American church planting statistics, but extends the illustrations to include worldwide church planting. More than anything else, this book will provide practical solutions for those planting churches today. Comiskey's book is a must-read book for all those interested in establishing Christ-honoring, multiplying churches. 176 pgs.

The Relational Disciple: *How God Uses Community to Shape Followers of Jesus*

Jesus lived with His disciples for three years and taught them life lessons as a group. After three years, he commanded them to "go and do likewise" (Matthew 28:18-20). Jesus discipled His followers through relationships—and He wants us to do the same. Scripture is full of exhortations to love and serve one another. This book will show you how. The isolation present in the western world is creating a hunger for community and the world is longing to see relational disciples in action. This book will encourage Christ-followers to allow God to use the natural relationships in life--family, friends, work relationships, cells, church, and missions to mold them into relational disciples.

You Can Coach: *How to Help Leaders Build Healthy Churches through Coaching*

We've entitled this book "You Can Coach" because we believe that coaching is more about passing on what you've lived and holding others accountable in the process. Coaching doesn't require a higher degree, special talent, unique personality, or a particular spiritual gift. We believe, in fact, that God wants coaching to become a movement. We long to see the day in which every pastor has a coach and in turn is coaching someone else. In this book, you'll hear three coaches who have successfully coached pastors for many years. They will share their history, dreams, principles, and what God is doing through coaching. Our hope is that you'll be both inspired and resourced to continue your own coaching ministry in the years to come.

INDEX

A

Abe Huber 81, 83
Africa 25, 55
Albert Einstein 79
Anabaptist 30
Anne White 9
Antioch Community Church 166
AWANA 66

B

Babe Ruth 79
baptism 188
Baptist 11, 23, 68, 75, 137, 182
Ben Wong 19, 21, 23, 128, 181
Bible 2, 4, 9, 30, 31, 50, 56, 59,
 60, 66, 71, 77, 87, 114,
 176, 182
biblical theology 48, 51
biblical truths 30, 49
Big Bear Christian Center 98,
 113, 136

Bill Beckham 27, 43, 45, 93, 175
Bill Joukhadar 9
Bob Roberts, Jr 167, 183
body of Christ 72, 93, 95, 105,
 114, 115, 129
Brazil 41, 91, 92, 93, 115
Brian McLemore 9
Brookside Free Methodist
 Church 114

C

California 55, 71, 136
Carl George 27
celebration 15, 16, 22, 26, 27,
 34, 38, 39, 72, 74, 85, 93,
 94, 96, 100, 113, 133, 143,
 144, 163, 165, 169, 170,
 171, 172, 173, 174, 175,
 178, 183
cell 185, 186, 187, 188, 189, 190,
 191, 192
Cell Church 185, 187, 192

197

147, 148, 149, 150, 151,
  158, 182, 189
coaching care structure 34
Colombia 32, 134
Comiskey 185, 186, 187, 188,
  189, 190, 191, 192
commission 89
community 50, 59, 60, 84, 98,
  107, 108, 109, 110, 111,
  113, 114, 118, 120, 126,
  127, 128, 166
counter-cultural 51
Count von Zinzendorf 16
CrossPoint Community Church
  87
Crossroads 109
Cultural sensitivity 58

D

David Cho 16, 27, 33, 125, 139,
  148, 166, 167
David Olson 25
Devotional 187
disciple 16, 25, 49, 78, 82, 83, 85,
  87, 88, 89, 98, 111, 130,
  134
disciple-maker 5, 7, 25, 87, 89
disciples 15, 24, 39, 49, 50, 57,
  59, 82, 83, 84, 85, 87, 89,
  92, 98, 126, 129, 141, 142,
  164, 168, 170, 180
discipleship 34, 82, 83, 89, 133,
  156, 157, 164, 165
Discover 185, 189, 191
Donald McGavran 55
Dr. Penrose St. Amant 11
Dwight Marble 98, 146, 182

cell church leaders 19, 65
Cell Church Legalism 5, 76
cell church literature 44, 77, 131
Cell Church Missions Network
  21
cell church vision 67, 68, 154
Cell Definition 5, 97
cell group 16, 33, 34, 47, 71, 74,
  75, 76, 77, 86, 88, 89, 97,
  101, 102, 103, 108, 109,
  110, 111, 112, 113, 115,
  118, 119, 121, 122, 130,
  134, 138, 140, 141, 144,
  146, 151, 153, 154, 155,
  157, 158, 161, 169
cell leaders 16, 40, 67, 71, 73, 77,
  83, 85, 105, 114, 124, 128,
  132, 135, 140, 141, 142,
  144, 148, 149, 181, 185,
  187, 188, 189
cell members 33, 83, 103, 105,
  111, 113, 114, 121, 122,
  123, 124, 128, 132, 133,
  142, 144
Challenging 189
Christ-followers 109, 168
Christian and Missionary Alliance
  135
Christian Reformed 170, 183
Christian Schwarz 168, 183
Christoph Schalk 177, 183
church building 34, 98
church planting 26, 44, 46, 68,
  123, 166, 172, 175, 179
coach 17, 39, 47, 51, 67, 77, 87,
  89, 122, 144, 147, 149,
  150, 151, 183, 185, 189
coaching 2, 34, 39, 40, 67, 71, 75,
  76, 77, 78, 87, 145, 146,

Index

E

ecclesiology 172
Ecuador 46, 47, 52, 68, 75, 76, 111, 134, 141, 160, 161, 173
Elim Church 31, 33, 57, 102, 103, 121, 122, 160, 191
El Salvador 31, 57, 134
Encounter 185, 188
Ephesians 12, 72, 104, 115
ESPN 150
Europe 25, 132
evangelism 12, 35, 49, 59, 88, 98, 110, 111, 117, 118, 119, 120, 121, 123, 124, 125, 126, 127, 128, 129, 130, 132, 156, 188
Evangelism Explosion 66
evangelistic outreach 120, 124, 158

F

fad 27, 48
Faith Community Baptist Church 137, 182
fallacy 20
Fuller Seminary 166

G

G12 32, 36, 148
Gailyn Van Rheenan 55
Gifts 191
Great Depression 15
group evangelism 188
Groups of Twelve 32, 35, 182, 185, 190
Grow 185, 186, 187, 188

Guatemala 57

H

Hadaway, S. Wright and DuBose 95
harvest 20, 55, 57, 86, 87, 124, 125, 129, 135, 136, 168
Henry Cloud 78
Holy Spirit 12, 50, 53, 98, 164
homogenous 100, 101
Honduras 134, 144
Hong Kong 19, 128
house churches 33, 49, 85, 95, 97, 166, 181

I

Igreja de Paz 83
International Charismatic Mission 32, 35, 100, 134

J

Jamey Miller 77
Japan 172
Jesus Christ 34, 37, 40, 51, 53, 96, 100, 101, 121, 130, 136, 164
Jim Corley 87, 88, 89
Jim Egli 98, 147, 182
Jimmy Seibert 166
Joel Comiskey 1, 2, 8, 12, 177, 178, 181, 182
John Mallison 95, 182
John Maxwell 78
John P. Kotter 37
John Townsend 78
John Wesley 16, 27
Joseph H. Hellerman 60

K

Ken Brown 120
Korea 22, 33, 167

L

Latin America 47, 77
Lawrence Khong 74, 182
leadership 188, 189, 190
Leadership Explosion 185, 188
Les Brickman 63, 65
Lewis and Clark 112
Listening 189
Live 185, 188
Lordship of Jesus 41
Luke 44, 45, 69, 87, 129

M

Mario Vega 29, 31, 57, 73, 122
Martin Luther 11
McDonalds 124
mega-cell churches 22, 23, 167
Mega-Church 3, 21, 22
Mega-Church Status 3, 22
Methodist 16, 27, 114, 115
Michael Jordan 39
Microsoft 50, 51
missionary 16, 46, 65, 135, 169
missions 169, 192
model 21, 29, 30, 31, 32, 33, 35, 36, 44, 45, 56, 65, 67, 69, 70, 71, 83, 87, 92, 93, 100, 148, 154, 158, 159
Moravian movement 16
multiplication 20, 34, 39, 49, 51, 59, 83, 84, 88, 98, 110, 122, 126, 127, 131, 132, 133, 134, 135, 136, 137, 139, 140, 141, 142, 143, 144, 168, 169, 170, 178, 179, 182
multi-site ministry 26

N

National Parks 15
Natural Church Development 25, 177, 178, 181, 183
New Testament 27, 31, 49, 54, 59, 60, 61, 95, 189, 191
North America 22, 24, 25, 47, 50, 52, 59, 60, 172, 177, 180, 191

O

Organic Growth 4, 52

P

pastor 11, 16, 17, 23, 24, 31, 32, 34, 37, 47, 48, 52, 53, 55, 56, 57, 58, 60, 67, 68, 70, 71, 72, 73, 74, 75, 76, 77, 78, 81, 82, 83, 85, 87, 89, 109, 113, 122, 123, 125, 133, 136, 137, 140, 141, 142, 147, 157, 158, 159, 160, 161, 166, 167, 170, 171, 172, 175, 176, 183
pastoral care 34
Patricia Barrett 9
Persistence 185, 191
Philippines 136
Philipp Spener 16
Phil Potter 69, 160
pilot group 158, 159, 160
pitfalls 17
potential leader 35, 140

Index

priesthood of all believers 30, 49
Prototype 7, 159
public worship 44, 171
Puerto Rico 74, 130
Puritans 30

R

Rae Holt 9
Rafer Johnson 79
Ralph Neighbour 27, 47, 48, 174, 175, 183, 191
Ralph W. Neighbour 13
Raymond Ebbett 135
Relational evangelism 124
relationships 99, 108, 110, 114, 115, 118, 119, 123, 143, 144, 157
René Molina 122
Reproduction 34
Republic Church 75, 76
Resources by Joel Comiskey 185
Richard Houle 68
Rob Campbell 10
Robert Lay 91, 93, 115
Rob Hastings 113
Ron Trudinger 26, 27
Russia 60

S

Samuel Mejia 71
Scott Boren 2, 10, 155, 161, 191
seeker models 26
Sergio Solorzano 160
Shekinah 40
Shepherd Community Church 21, 128
Singapore 137, 182
small group ministry 15, 110, 130, 146, 161
small groups 45, 94, 111 187, 191
South Africa 55
Spain 134, 135
spiritual gifts 191
Spiritual gifts 95
Steep Learning Curve 67
Steve Cordle 10, 109
Stuart Gramenz 111
Switzerland 133, 135

T

Ted Haggard 97
testimony 41, 68, 118, 119
Thomas Edison 79
Touch Outreach 119
traditional church 12, 55, 153, 158, 187
Traditional Ministry 5, 73, 74
Traditional models 45
Training 39, 97, 189
training track 39, 47, 78, 86, 88, 89, 121, 140, 141, 143, 157
transformation 191
transition 26, 68, 69, 153, 154, 155, 156, 158, 159, 160, 161, 187
Trinity 50
Tucson, Arizona 87

U

unbelievers 12, 119, 120

V

Vacation Bible School 66

W

Werner Kniesel 133, 135
Windows DOS 50
Winston Churchill 79
World War II 141

Y

Yoido Full Gospel Church 125, 167
Yosemite 15